Child's Play in the Seasons

CHILD'S PLAY IN THE SEASONS

Jean Ellen and Barbara Blake
in Wintertime

JEAN KING

Illustrations by Ann Morrissey Davidson

BLUFF STREET CORNER AND
FOULDS AVENUE PRESS
ALTON, ILLINOIS 2024

THIS BOOK IS PUBLISHED BY
JEAN KING

COPYRIGHT 2024

ALL RIGHTS RESERVED.
NO PART OF THIS BOOK MAY BE USED OR
REPRODUCED IN ANY MEANS WHATSOEVER
WITHOUT WRITTEN PERMISSION.

ISBN 979-8-35095-426-5

Printed by BookBaby Publishing
Manufactured in the United States of America

FOR OUR FAMILY
AND
ANY INTERESTED READERS

CONTENTS

Introduction
84 ½

Spring
One: The First Day of Spring 1
Two: Growing Pains 5
Three: Roses and Canadian Bacon 11
Four: Flooding and the Indians 13
Five: Friendly Thunder 19
Six: The Swing 21
Seven: The Hollow 25

Summer View from the Curb 31
Eight: The First Rose of Summer 33
Nine: Ins and Outs 37
Ten: Ah-choo! 41
Eleven: Play Ball! 45
Twelve: James Joseph King 51
Thirteen: Sunday Mornings 55
Fourteen: Rituals 63

Autumn "Olly Olly Oxen Free!" 69
Fifteen: A Timely Lesson 73
Sixteen: Good Stock 77
Seventeen: Marie Antoinette Morrissey 81
Eighteen: Dial 37531 85

Winter
Nineteen: Prospect Street 91
Twenty: The Ice Cutters 97
Christmas 101

All Seasons A Guy for All Seasons
The Whistler 105

Introduction

When my family moved from 400 Prospect Street in 1955, I didn't think a thing about it. At seventeen, I had no sentimental feelings about the house, nor any appreciation of the extraordinary childhood my parents had given my sister and me. I had taken a happy home for granted.

I don't even remember the actual moving day, any preparations for the move, or who bought our house. I only remember that the three of us, Mom, Pop, and I, moved to an upstairs apartment at 1203 State Street in Alton. My sister, Barbara, had married the year before. Aunt Helen Morrissey and her two children, Jean Louise and Gene, who also had lived at 400 Prospect Street, moved to Helen's mother's home on Forest Home Place in Alton.

A short time later, my Father suffered a fatal heart attack on the morning of December 29, 1955 and died that evening at St. Joseph's Hospital. As a consequence, my Mother and Aunt Helen decided to bring our families together again as we had lived on Prospect Street. So Mom and I, and Aunt Helen and her two children moved into the Lauer apartments at 519 Henry Street.

When Jean Louise, Gene, and I left home, my Mother moved to Winamac, Indiana, to "be with Barbara and the children," and Aunt Helen moved to an apartment on Henry Street next door to where the Morrisseys and Kings had lived together as one family.

84 ½

You know how when you're little and someone asks you how old you are, and you proudly answer in the halves because you just can't wait to grow up?

"How old are you, little girl?"
"4 ½"

Well, to keep the tradition alive,
"Go ahead, ask me, and
I'll proudly tell you."

"How old are you, Jean Ellen?"
"84 1/2"

"84 1/2! So what've you been doing for 84 1/2 years?"

Now it's my turn to pose the question.
"Do you really want to know?"

"Sure do!"

"Then read on!"

Child's Play in the Seasons

CHILD'S PLAY IN THE SEASONS

Spring

ONE   THE FIRST DAY OF SPRING

The March winds of 1938 whirl across the Mississippi River, sweep over the bluffs and shoot straight up the hollow to our house on Prospect Street. It's the 25th day of the month, and I've just been born on the heels of my Father's birthday, a fact which will confound me for most of my childhood. How can he, who's so much bigger than me, be only four days older?

Each year, when we celebrate our birthdays, my dilemma resurfaces, but my family's answers, like my question, remain the same. "The day you figure that one out, kiddo," Pop tells me, his stomach jiggling with stifled laughter as I sit there on his lap, "we'll have a party just to celebrate it. You just have to get that one little brain cell of yours to work harder," he teases, lightly tapping my head. The grin on his face sports the immense pleasure he derives from my puzzlement.

For my Mother, there's no dilemma. With the sweep of her hand, she dismisses my question. "Here, try drying this plate while you're standing there thinking about it," she scoffs, handing me a dishtowel. For the moment, at least, Mom makes my quandary seem not such a big deal after all.

Even Gramps can't rescue me, though he tries. "When you grow up, little girl," he says, patting the top of my head, consolingly, "then you'll understand." But his response only intensifies my confusion. How come Pop got bigger than me in only four days?

"Daddy was born on the first day of Spring," my sister, Barbara, triumphantly declares, like that will explain everything. She has, of course, hit the raw nerve of my dilemma—the first day of Spring. Somehow, in the four days preceding my birth, my Father, like Jack in the Beanstalk, got all the way grown.

So on and on it goes, until, like my Winter clothes, I store away my dilemma until next year and another birthday.

It's March again, and my Father tells me that the St. Louis Cardinals are heading south to Florida to begin Spring training. His passion for baseball is contagious. Already, I hear the crack of the bat and the cheering fans, and my taste buds water just thinking of the hot dogs I'll consume during the seventh inning stretch.

"Let's go!" I holler, and am halfway out the door.

"Not so fast, kiddo," he laughs, "it's only Spring training, not the games." Seeing my disappointment, he explains. "Every team has to practice first before the season opens to get in shape after the long Winter. It won't take long, though, and once those Red Birds start swinging their bats, we'll go watch 'em hit the balls right out of the ballpark and into the World Series!" Then he reaches into his pocket and pulls out a battered baseball signed by Cardinal players from last season. "Want me to show you how to pitch a fast ball?" he asks. And together, we're out the door.

Life is like baseball, my Father seems to be telling me. First you practice so you can play a good game, and then, if you keep at it, you're sure to win. So I figure, if I keep trying, I'll solve my dilemma about birthdays—maybe this year. Admiringly, I look all the way up to him. He's smart even, I'm thinking.

I bet that's how he got to be so much bigger than me in just four days in the first place.

TWO   GROWING PAINS

"Has anyone seen my Eversharp pencil?" Mom calls up the kitchen steps.
"Jean Ellen had it this morning when she measured herself in the kitchen," Barbara hollers back.
"Is she upstairs there with you?"
"No."
"Heaven knows where she put it!"

All along the side of the house, forsythia shine golden in the freshness of Springtime. Clusters of yellow and purple crocuses dot our front yard like Easter eggs nestled in grass that's trying to turn green. Already, buds appear on the pair of persimmon trees to both sides of the walk. From the porch, empty stone urns, like mannequins, await their summer dress of red geraniums. Out

5

back, the old oak displays its first hint of foliage, while robins herald the season in song down in the hollow.

"Everything's growin,'" I tell Mom, "'cept me."

"Nonsense," she says, squaring her shoulders, "you're going to be nice and tall, just like your Mother. Here," and she hands me a cup and saucer to help set the dinner table. "Be careful with that cup."

Gingerly, I carry the items to the table. "But when?" I ask.

"Oh, heavens, Jean Ellen, you'll be grown before you know it, and then you'll wish you hadn't." My Mother laughs, but I don't know why.

"Four days?" I ask, hopefully.

"It'll take a little longer than that, but it'll all work out in the end." I look up at her, wondering. "Just remember to stand up straight and throw your shoulders back. You'll look worse if you stoop." Mom always says there's nothing worse than a tall woman who's round-shouldered. So I thrust out my chest, look up to the ceiling, and force my shoulders back.

"Like this?"

"That'll do."

Without changing my stance, I grope my way back to the counter and open the utensil drawer. Fumbling around inside, I come up with knife, fork, and spoon, and retrace my steps to the dining room table where I carefully arrange them. All the while, Mom's saying, "Look at all of Barbara Blake's hand-me-downs you can wear. They wouldn't fit if you hadn't grown into them." That makes me drop my stance and look myself over. It's true. Practically everything I have on once belonged to my sister. Before now, I hadn't felt happy getting all her old clothes.

"My new jacket used to be Barbara's, too," I add, feeling sudden pride.

My Mother smiles, looking down at me. "Do you know what the first sentence was you ever said?"

I shake my head, not wanting to guess.

"'Used to be Barbara's.'"

Then Mom takes her Eversharp pencil out of the kitchen drawer. "Come over here a minute," she says, so I follow her to the basement door. "Stand against the woodwork so I can mark how tall you are." Eagerly, I flatten myself against the frame of the door, pushing out my chest as far as it'll go. "Just stand up straight, Jean Ellen. You don't need to go through all those shenanigans. You'll grow up looking like the old lady who opened the window and threw out her chest." She pauses long enough to laugh at the saying she always enjoys repeating. Then I feel her hand brush the top of my head. "There!" she exclaims, and I move away to see the mark she has made. "Next week we'll measure again. Then you'll see for yourself how much you've grown. We can mark it all summer long, if you want. Before you know it, you'll be climbing up the wall just like Mrs. Springman's roses." I like the idea of growing up like our neighbor's roses 'cause everyone on Prospect Street knows Elizabeth Springman has the prettiest rose garden in the whole wide world.

The very next morning, I race down the steps to the kitchen, hold my finger to the mark and slip under it, hoping to push up my hand. But it doesn't even budge.

****

"Wait for me!" I shout at my sister as she takes off on her bike down the driveway. Moments later, I'm pushing my tricycle into the front yard as Mom appears on the front porch.

"Stay close to Jean Ellen," she tells her. "And don't go in the street with her."

"Oh, Mom," Barbara replies, annoyed. "I can hardly keep going, she peddles so slow." That makes me pucker up, so she says, "All right. Come on. But try to go faster, o.k.?" I climb up on the seat and begin pedaling, but my feet keep slipping off. Barbara stops her bike and looks back at me, scowling.

Jean Ellen with Barbara on tricycle

"Wait, honey," Mom says to her, coming down off the porch. "I'll walk alongside. Go toward Springman's. The walks are smoother up that way." So down the clickety-clack driveway we go, and, with Mom holding me on, swerve left onto the sidewalk, heading up Prospect Street. As we reach Springman's, our neighbor appears on her porch. Slowly, she waddles down her front walk to greet us.

"Taking your girls for a ride, Mrs. King?" she asks in her cheerful, cackling voice.

"Yes, Mrs. Springman," Mom replies. "Barbara Blake's being very patient while Jean Ellen learns to ride her tricycle."

Our neighbor chuckles. "So you're having to pedal around in circles until your little sister gets the hang of it, is that it, Barbara?"

"Yes, Mrs. Springman."

"My, oh my, Mrs. King," she exclaims, "they grow up right under your eyes, don't they? Before long, Barbara'll be teaching Jean Ellen to ride a bicycle."

"They certainly do, Mrs. Springman. The last time I saw JoAnn, I just couldn't believe how fast she's grown." JoAnn is the youngest of Joe and Elizabeth Springman's eight children.

"Joe thinks she's going to pass up her older sisters pretty soon. And before you know it," Mrs. Springman adds, cocking her head to one side and sizing me up, "Jean Ellen'll be peddling past here on her own, too." She motions toward my sister who's riding her bike in circles in the street, and lets out a cackle. "And I can see it won't come too soon for Barbara!"

Suddenly, I remember Mom saying that I'll grow like Mrs. Springman's roses, so I ask, "Can I see your roses, Mrs. Springman?"

"I was telling Jean Ellen that she'll grow up as fast as your beautiful roses," Mom explains.

"Oh," Mrs. Springman laughs, delighted with the mention of her rose garden. "It isn't time for the roses yet, Jean Ellen. Give them a few more weeks, then come on over to the backyard and I'll show you. Around mid-to-late June is when they start."

THREE ROSES AND CANADIAN BACON

The delicious aroma of Canadian bacon from Springman's kitchen floats over Mrs. Green's backyard and up to our bedroom. It signals Sunday morning 'cause the Springmans always have Canadian bacon on Sundays. All at once, I have an urge to go check on Mrs. Springman's roses.

Minutes later, I'm on tiptoe ringing their front doorbell. Pressing my nose against the screen door, I see gold chimes hanging in the hallway like the organ pipes at the Cathedral. "Come on in," someone calls from inside, and as I open the door, JoAnn and the Springman's border collie, Tippy, meet me in the hall.

"Is it time for the roses yet?" I ask, patting the dog.

"Oh, you better ask Mother about that," JoAnn tells me. "Come on in the kitchen. She's fixing breakfast." Tippy runs on ahead of us, her nose fast on the Canadian bacon trail.

11

All year, it's Springtime inside the Springman home. Flowers are displayed everywhere—in the wallpaper, divan and chairs, even the dining room curtains present a floral design. In the kitchen, Mrs. Springman stands over the stove frying the Canadian bacon in her flowered dress and apron.

"Jean Ellen wants to see the rose garden," JoAnn tells her mother.

"It's still too soon for that," Mrs. Springman says, looking over her shoulder at me. "You're welcome to look outside, if you want, but there's nothing to see. Not for a couple more weeks, Jean Ellen." I nod, my eyes glued to the skillet where the Canadian bacon sizzles. She follows my stare. "Want to have some breakfast?"

"Yes, Mrs. Springman!" I emphatically reply.

"Just take a seat over there at the table then. JoAnn, get a plate and some utensils for Jean Ellen."

Eagerly, I pull a chair up to their round kitchen table in the corner. There's sure nothing better than being in Mrs. Springman's kitchen on Sunday morning with Canadian bacon coming my way. Like Pop says about baseball, this is the best seat in the house, 'cause from where I'm sitting, I can keep a close watch on Mrs. Springman's rose garden out the back door and eat Canadian bacon at the same time.

FOUR   FLOODING AND THE INDIANS

I wake to the sound of coffee percolating downstairs in the kitchen. Rolling out of bed, I sleepily head down the back steps, knowing that where there's coffee, food can't be far behind.

"Every Spring the same dern thing happens," I hear Mom saying. "You'd think by now somebody'd realize that downtown's built too close to the river."

"Not much I can do about that, Annie," my Father replies. "Alton wouldn't know it's Spring without the Mississippi flooding."

"What's 'flooding'?" I ask, tripping off the steep bottom step into the kitchen.

My parents look at one another but neither answers. "Good morning, sleepy head," my Father says as he folds up the *Alton Telegraph*, and motions for me to join him at the table. I stand on tiptoe to see the batter Mom's mixing in the bowl, then clumsily climb up on a chair next to him, pulling the tablecloth askew in my struggle to get seated. "Careful, kiddo, don't spill the coffee. Here," and he places his glass of orange juice in front of me.

But I'll not be deterred. "What's 'flooding'?" I ask again.

13

Pop shoots a look at Mom who deflects him. "That's your department, Jimmie," she says, as she pours batter into the waffle iron. My Father puts his coffee cup in the saucer and sits back in his chair, observing me. From my experience of four years, I know that I'm in for a long explanation.

"Remember all the snow we had this Winter?" he begins.

"Yeah."

"Well, it didn't snow just in Alton. Snow fell on the mountains far up the river in Wisconsin and Minnesota, too. And now that Spring's here, the snow's melting and running down the mountainsides into the Mississippi, but the river can't hold it all so it runs over..."

"Runs over?" I break in, and my lips begin to quiver because I see my pet lying on Prospect Street that Sunday morning last summer, hit by a car. "Like Wiggles?" I cry out.

"Oh, no, kiddo," Pop hastily adds, apologetically, "not 'runs over' like a car. Not that kind of runs over. I should have said 'spills over,' like if you knocked over your orange juice. The river spills over."

"Oh," I scrunch back in my chair, careful to hold the juice glass tight, and sip. Still, I persist with my questions. "Spills over where?"

"Jimmie, maybe you should change the subject," Mom says as she lights the burner under the bacon frying pan.

But I'm all ears now, wanting to know more about the river flooding and spilling over. So I keep at it.

"Where does it spill over, Pop?"

"Its banks. Sometimes the river gets so swollen that it spills over the sides of the banks, and that's what we call flooding."

Seeing my eyes large with fear now as I begin to grasp what flooding means, he tries to soothe me. "Look, kiddo," he says, "we live way up here on the bluffs, don't we? Just think how high the water'd have to get to spill over into Summit Street." Slowly, I nod, knowing how steep that street is where we sled every Winter. "And Prospect Street's even higher than Summit. We're very lucky to live up here because the bluffs protect us from flooding."

Pleased with his explanation to calm my fears, Pop smiles as Mom puts a plate of waffles, eggs and bacon in front of him. "I fixed a good breakfast this morning because I know you and Ed have a long day ahead of you," she tells him.

"The city put sandbags all around the riverbank, kiddo, but the water was still too high and it spilled over them," Pop goes on as he helps himself to the breakfast plate.

"Sandbags?" I ask. "What's sandbags?"

"You sure are full of questions this morning, Jean Ellen," Mom exclaims. "Give your Father a chance to eat his breakfast."

But Pop laughs. "Guess now's as good a time as any for a little lesson, eh, kiddo? Sandbags are big, tough bags made out of burlap that we fill to protect us from the river running ov…I mean, from the river spilling over into…into…" My Father hesitates, and the kitchen becomes quiet except for the sound of the Aunt Jemima syrup bottle Mom sets on the table.

"Into where?" I ask.

My Father nervously meets my gaze. After a long pause, he says, "Well, kiddo, it spills into—downtown." And he says it like those were the last words he'd ever want to utter. He stares into his coffee cup and Mom sits down so cautiously that I think she's sitting on egg shells. His shoulders sag, and I see he's worried. "It has, in fact, already flooded the entire West Third Street business district. And," he glumly adds, "Morrissey-King Shoes."

"Wow!" I exclaim. All at once I see the mighty Mississippi careening out of control, gushing all over the sidewalks and streets downtown—Block's maraschino cherry ice cream sundaes and Thrifty's Double Bubble gum all floating away! In a flash, I plunk the juice glass on the table, slide off my chair and race toward the back steps.

"Where are you going, Jean Ellen?" Mom calls after me, startled. "Don't you want your breakfast?"

"I'll be right back, Mom!" I holler excitedly, halfway up the steps. "I gotta get my galoshes!"

My parents burst out laughing, and I hear the relief in my Mother's voice when she calls up the stairs, "What on earth for?"

"We can't walk in town if that's what you're thinking," Pop hollers. "The water's too deep even with your galoshes on." I stop at the top of the steps, perplexed. "But," he adds, looking up at me now from below, "we can go through in a rowboat. That's how I'm getting to the store. How'd you like to do that, kiddo?" I forget about galoshes and hurry back down the steps.

"Now don't get her hopes up, Jimmie," Mom tells him as I climb back up to the table for the breakfast I nearly missed. "Ed told you they're not letting anyone go through town except store owners."

"Right, but they'll let the girls in with me." Turning to me, he says, "So now you know what 'flooding' means, eh, kiddo?" I nod vigorously as Mom cuts a waffle into pieces on my plate. "But what I want you to remember is that you and your sister are always safe because we live way up here on the bluffs, and the water never gets this high."

"The Indians had more sense than us," Mom puts in. "They wouldn't think of building dams or anything that'd change the course of the river. Businessmen should have figured that out, too, before they built so close to it."

"Well, like I said, not much we can do about that, Annie," Pop tells her, a trace of irritation in his voice. "Without the river to transport goods, people couldn't have made a living in the old days."

But Mom ignores his remark and looks out the window at the Mississippi instead. "I still think they had more sense."

My Father drains his coffee cup and sets it back in the saucer. "Finish your breakfast, Jean Ellen, then go find your sister and we'll leave for the store. Like your Mother said, your Uncle Ed and I have a lot of work to do."

Later that morning, like explorers Marquette and Joliet, Barb and I join our Father in paddling a rowboat through flooded West Third Street in downtown Alton.

I see our reflections rowing the boat in the display windows of Vogue Women's Apparel, Kresge's Five & Ten Cent Store, and Young's Department Store. Eagerly, I scan the water surface for ice cream floating out of Block's or gum from Thrifty's up Belle Street. It's like steering the boats at the Highlands Amusement Park in St. Louis, except over there the water's clear and black; here, there's nothing but the muddy Mississippi, and that, Barb says, isn't even good enough for mud pies 'cause you don't know what all's in it. Still, it's much more fun rowing downtown in a boat than walking. But as we row through the entrance of our store, suddenly it doesn't feel like fun anymore.

Inside, the water's almost up to the cash register, and shoe boxes, like pickup sticks, are piled helter-skelter everywhere. Uncle Ed Morrissey appears out of the back in a rowboat. He's not grinning like usual, though. He doesn't even say hello. All he says is, "Haven't got a prayer back there, Jim. No sense bringing more boxes out; there's no place to stack them. We'll just have to wait 'til the river recedes. The *Telegraph* says it'll take another week, if we're lucky."

"I brought the two best helpers I could find," my Father says, trying to sound cheerful. My uncle looks at us, like it's the first time he realizes Barb and I are there, and rows closer.

"You girls having fun?"

"Yeah!" we respond, but he doesn't seem to hear 'cause he's staring past us out the front door at the water, which is everywhere.

"All the snow slided off the mountains," I tell him, in case he's wondering about 'flooding'. Still, he just sits there like in a trance. "It spilled over the sandbags but they couldn't mop it all up or anything and it didn't have to happen if we did like the Indians 'cause they would never build their tents downtown 'cause they were smart and they knew flooding didn't go up the bluffs." Uncle Ed looks at me now, a blank expression on his face. He puts down his oars and stares at me.

"Yeah," Barb chimes in. "Mother says the Indians had sense. They stayed up on the bluffs not on the riverbank."

"Like us!" I exclaim, suddenly feeling a jolt of understanding.

A long silence ensues before Uncle Ed responds in a drawl as long as the river itself. "Is that so?" He looks out the front door again. "Well, I wish one of those smart Indians would paddle their canoe in here right now and help us figure out where the—where to move all these shoes."

My sister looks at me and shrugs. From the expression on our uncle's face, something tells us he doesn't think much of our story about flooding and the Indians.

Just then, Barb perks up, her eyes sparkling with clarity. "They couldn't do that, Uncle Ed," she explains. "They wouldn't know what shoes are. Everyone knows Indians wear moccasins."

FIVE FRIENDLY THUNDER

A bolt of lightning flashes across the April sky, lighting up the front yard. Huddled in a corner of the porch swing, I peep out from under the pillow I so earnestly hug.

The screen door opens. "Well, well, look who's out on the porch all by herself in this thunderstorm!" Grandpa exclaims. Sitting beside me, he wraps an arm around my shoulder. "Are you afraid, little girl?"

A clap of thunder buries me deep in his side, as he tosses the pillow aside. Lightning illuminates the sky again, and in a few seconds, thunder rocks the swing, followed by a series of rolls fading into the distance.

"There, now," Grandpa says, letting go of me, "it's all over, at least for a little while." I look up at him, reluctant to leave his side especially after hearing that last part about a little while. "One good thing about thunder," he tells me, "you always know when it's coming."

"How?" I anxiously ask, hoping he hurries up and explains before the next boom.

"Lightning always precedes it," he says, smiling confidently down at me. Upon seeing the question still on my face, he rephrases his statement. "In other words, first comes the lightning, then the thunder. So just remember, whenever you see lightning in the sky, prepare yourself, because thunder will follow right on its heels."

"Oh," I remark, looking up at the sky more confidently now. But the clouds have turned a sickening green and the grass in the front yard is flooded in a yellowish hue. It's not long before lightning cuts another jagged streak across the sky. I lunge into Gramps' side, and this time hold my ears anticipating the crack of thunder.

"Here it comes!" he exclaims, tightening his grip around me. Bam! The crash nearly knocks me off the swing. "That was a close call!" he admits in a thin voice, and I realize that he, too, got a little scared. He wraps me closer in his arms. "But remember, little girl, thunder will never hurt you, it's your friend. It warns you that a storm is on its way, and if you're out playing, you need to come inside."

Just then, Mom appears at the screen door. "Mrs. Springman just called to say Tippy's hiding somewhere in the house and she can't find her!" Tippy, our neighbor's border collie, hates thunder because it hurts her ears. Mom looks out at the rain which is coming down steadily now. "Putting screens up on the porch was the best idea Jimmie ever had!" she says. "It gives you kids a place to play on rainy days like this."

Like clockwork, my sister opens the door. "Oh, there you are, Jean Ellen!" and Mom holds the door to let her through. "Wanna play Jacks?" Without waiting for my reply, Barb scatters the game on the porch floor and I jump off the swing to join her.

Suddenly, lightning flashes across the sky, and I scramble back to the swing and Gramps' side. But this time, he covers my ears and I cover his, our eyes wide in expectation of the oncoming thunder. Bam! The powerful clap makes me jump as it rattles the picture window alongside us. But the scary part is over, so we uncover our ears just in time to hear thunder roll, like falling dominoes, far away up the Mississippi.

SIX   THE SWING

As if they haven't enough to do at the store after the flood, Mom says, Uncle Ed and my Father build a swing for Barb and me in between our house and our next door neighbors, the Kitzmillers.

The first morning after they finish it, I'm out of bed, down the back steps, out the kitchen door and climbing up on the seat. "YIPES!" I holler, leaping off the cold metal. In my haste, I forgot to put on underpants. Back to the house and up the steps I scamper, and run into Grandpa as he emerges from his bedroom.

"My, oh my!" he exclaims. "Did you forget something, little girl?"

"Yep!" I answer, racing past him into my room. Hurriedly, I pull on a pair of pants under my playsuit, and moments later am back on the swing. That's when I discover my feet don't touch the ground.

"Swing me," I plead in the silence of early morning. But inside, our house remains as still as all Prospect Street. I try again, "Grandpa, please swing me!"

"Shhh! You'll wake the whole neighborhood!" Mom hisses from the kitchen door. "E. J.'s having his breakfast. You'll have to wait 'til Barbara gets up," and she disappears into the house.

Minutes later, my sister sticks her head out the screen door. "Mom's slicing oranges if you want some," she tells me. Off the seat I scoot and stumble up the steps, but Barb, to my surprise, runs past me on her way down the steps.

"Wait for me, Barb," I plead, guessing where she's headed, and run inside.

"Catch the door," Mom cautions, "or you'll wake the Kitzmillers. How do you want your orange sliced? Regular or in boats?"

"Boats! Make 'em in boats and hurry up," I tell Mom as I eye my sister out there swinging into the sky.

"Is that an order?" Mom asks, giving me a sidelong glance. Collecting the pieces, she puts them in my hands. "Share them with Barbara, and be careful not to drop any on your way out," she says, as she opens the door for me. Cautiously, I retrace my steps, the orange sections wobbling in my hands. Reaching the bottom step, I quickly lick all the "boats," and not too soon.

"Can I have a piece?" Barb asks, coming to a halt on the swing.

"Sure," I reply, holding one out to her, "but I already licked it."

"Ugh!" she cries out in disgust, and jumps off the swing, running back inside.

I sit down on the sidewalk, setting the orange slices beside me, and squeeze them, one by one, slurping the sweet juice as fast as I can. Most days, the peelings make great boats in the dirt where the swing now stands, but this morning, I turn them into shovels, scooping up dirt from under the seat. Then I stack up the pebbles, drawing circles in the dirt around them.

Suddenly, I realize I'm on to something. Running inside, I get Mom's favorite mixing spoon, and a minute later am back under the swing digging—digging for hell. Somewhere deep down in the earth the pebbles will give way to a huge boulder that marks the entrance to the inferno, and when I hit on it, I'll know I've arrived. Lucky for me, the rock will keep me safe from the raging fires beneath it.

"What are you doing out there?" Mom calls from the kitchen door. I've been quiet too long.

"Just playing," I evasively reply.

"Do it some place else," my Mother says, coming out on the porch now to get a better look. "You'll have holes all over the place where you swing."

"Okay." But I just sit there in the dirt, feeling content in my secret that I can come here anytime and know the rock will protect me from the raging fires below.

When Pop and Grandpa come home from work that evening, they take turns pushing me on the swing. Pop pushes me so hard that the rope loops and I'm off the seat, suspended in air, feeling like my stomach just left my body. Even Gramps, although cautious at first, nearly flings me over the low side of Kitzmiller's roof.

Before my sister and I go in for the night, she shows me how to start on my own by scooting down on the seat and pushing with my foot to get a good start. Soon I'll pump all by myself, Barb says, and not have to ask for someone to swing me. I'll pump so hard that I'll make my own loops in the air, and see clear over the hollow to Bailey's house any time I want to. I'll just swing and swing, like on a seesaw, for as long as I want.

SEVEN   THE HOLLOW

It is about 9:00 in the morning when I see him coming down the path behind his house to the hollow. Far over the ridge he looks small as a stick man, but I know who he is. Even at a distance I can see the hoe on his shoulder and the spade in his hand and the rickety old wheelbarrow he pushes. I recognize the decisive yet unsteady gait, the latter due to age more than intention. Presently, he drops out of sight under the ridge, but I can imagine him crossing over the long stretch of path that leads directly up the rugged incline to the top. As he comes into view, I see his huge overall pockets bulging with packets of seedlings, and the rickety old cart he has filled with gunny sacks and smaller tools. From his suspenders hang a pair of spectacles. A red bandana, held fast by the cap on his head, wraps around his forehead in wake of the inevitable sweat of his labors. From where I stand in my backyard, the sight of Mr. Bailey coming to plant our vegetable garden in the hollow ushers in Spring.

    I weave my way through the forsythia that already blossoms along the side of our house, hurry past the old oak, and jump off the backyard wall onto the path to meet him. I know the path well. At the top of the hill it skims close to the wall, then dips down, makes a quick upturn, winds downward again to the left, the steepest part, and then levels off into the hollow. The early May sun is already warm on my arms, and as I hurry along the path, I can smell Spring in the air. Not that the hollow is resplendent with flowers, for it is not. It is quite ordinary, mostly grass and shrubs on our side, anyway. Nothing fancy. But an array of birds sing high in the trees that protect our vegetable garden where I know Mr. Bailey is headed. It is a good place for a garden, Mom told me, because the trees shade part of it on the south side while the rest of it gets plenty of sun. Best of all, the level ground prevents rain from running off.

I can hear the old wheelbarrow bumping along now as Mr. Bailey works his way across the floor of the hollow over the rugged, tangled brush. Upon seeing me, he smiles, nods, and sets down the cart with a grunt.

"Come to help, Jean Ellen?" he asks in his gruff voice, but I know from other times that he is a gentle man.

"Yes, Mr. Bailey," I shyly answer.

The old man nods his assent, straightens his cap, and lets out a low whistle as he surveys the uncultivated garden spot covered with mulch. I know he is thinking of the work ahead of him, just like last Spring when I had watched him, for the first time, plant the garden. He is smart, though, this Mr. Bailey. Last Fall he had dumped hay all over the area "to keep the soil protected in Winter," he had explained, adding, "Next Spring, we'll turn 'er under." I haven't forgotten the excitement I felt when he said "we'll." Mom had warned me not to "get in Mr. Bailey's way." So his inclusion told me I hadn't, and that he wanted me to help him this Spring.

"Now, Jean Ellen, help me work this ol' Winter coat in," he says, pointing to the mulch strewn before us. I grin up at him, trying to hide my uncertainty about what to do. "Just watch me," he says, as he grabs a spade from the wheelbarrow and breaks up clods of dirt. Then he thrusts the spade upright in the ground, takes a shovel, and folds the mulch under. "Just like that," he tells me, and he does it again, just to be sure I get the hang of it. This tool he also stands in the ground while he searches around in the wheelbarrow. "Ah!" he suddenly exclaims, retrieving something from under the gunny sacks. "Here we are!" He motions me over, holding up a hand hoe, and gives it to me.

Back to the garden we go, Bailey breaking up the earth and rolling it over, and I folding in any mulch he misses, just like Mom does with egg whites when baking her delicious lemon meringue pies. That thought spurs me on, as I eagerly fold the mulch into the earth. "That's right, keep goin' just like you're doin'," Mr. Bailey tells me, as a chuckle escapes him.

At length, we are working up a sweat. Well, Mr. Bailey more than me, but he is a kindly and patient man who doesn't mind as I struggle to keep up with him. Eventually, we fall into rhythm like a metronome, back and forth, him spading and me folding. We work most of the morning that way until Mom comes down the hollow path with coffee for Mr. Bailey, lemonade for me, and cookies for us both.

"Jean Ellen's not in your way, is she, Mr. Bailey?" Mom asks.

"Oh, no, Mrs. King," he replies. Gratefully, he takes the cup and saucer from her. "She's been quite the little helper, I'd say!"

Mom laughs, pleased with his kind reply. "Well, just so she doesn't get under your feet."

Clarence Bailey has farmed his whole life, even a six-year-old like me can see that. My family was fortunate the day he offered to plant and care for our vegetable garden. With my Father busy at the store, and Mom with housework, his offer was a welcome one. In lots of ways he reminds me of old Mr. Flynn, a family friend. Many summer suns shine in his tanned face, the air of all seasons in his clear, blue eyes, and the reward of hard work in his huge, leathery hands. My family's not like that, I sometimes think, though I know my parents respect the soil and the people who work it. We're city folk. Yet just like my parents, I love going to visit the Flynns on their farm. As I ponder the thought, I become aware that Mr. Bailey is quietly looking down at me.

That Spring, Mr. Bailey and I develop a bond much like the one with the plants we tend. I try my best to do as he directs, and he, in turn, maintains a level of patience that should earn him a Gardener of the Year award. We plant, cultivate, weed, and even worry together if the rain doesn't come. I like the earthy smell of the soil that he lets me hold to my nose after he turns it over with his spade. Careful not to sniff in a worm that might live there, I breathe in through my nostrils for as long as I can, then exhale with such exaggeration that Mr. Bailey, amused, momentarily stops his hoeing and puts on his spectacles, just to watch. The best part, though, is when he lets me drop seeds in the rows he has so carefully prepared. Long rows he cultivates on the flat stretch of land below our house, and long hours he toils to make good the yield that eventually comes. And so it goes. We work until noon, then pack up the wagon and head over the ridge up the path to his house. I tag along holding the gunny sacks, but we both know it is only my excuse to stay longer in the hollow.

The hollow is comprised of two wide tracts of land divided by a high ridge that runs their length, south-northward, like the spine of some gigantic dinosaur. The land on the west side of the ridge is Bailey's side, and that to the east, ours. This is because two paths lead into the hollow: one from behind our backyard wall, and the other to the right of Bailey's farmhouse. The two paths lead directly into the hollow and run up the sides of the ridge where they meet at the top.

I can run and skip along the winding spine of that ridge, or roll down its ribs to either side. If I roll down Mr. Bailey's side, I bump down all the way because of terrace-like grooves that run lengthwise along the ribs and the holes that in some places flank its side. If I fall to our side, I don't go far because of the small bushes and tangled brush that grow there. If I walk the ridge far up its spine, I can come in through a neighbor's backyard. But the only "real" paths in the hollow are ours and Mr. Bailey's.

Just as the terrain varies on both sides of the ridge, so does the hollow's floor. So distinct, in fact, that when crossing over, you think you are passing from one part of the country to another. One minute you are in Illinois, the next in Kansas. On the Illinois, or our side, the hollow is flat, fertile for gardening, and partially shaded by trees. A wall divides our property from next door's, and a huge stone watering hole for cattle fills the corner at the end of their lot. The Kansas, or Bailey's, side of the hollow, is treeless, and, in the heat of summer, the grass scorches blond and the earth grinds down to a dustbowl. I can "hole up" in any number of dust bins that sit like pockets all along the rib of the ridge. With my friends, I play all day on that side, hunkering down in the holes, sporting long blades of grass in my teeth as I watch the barges lumber up and down the Mississippi. Very Tom and Huck-like. This side of the hollow had at one time been pasture; the entire character of the place testifies to it. I can imagine cows grazing along the hillside and coming home up the path to Bailey's. At one point midway to their house, the path is so worn that the ground rises on both sides to my waist.

The hollow offers the best of both worlds: the intimacy and satisfaction that comes from working the earth, and the expansion of possibilities that an open pasture suggests. I learn about the miracle of growing things, of paying attention to their natural order, of caring, and of yielding to situations not under my control. I am at home, stuffing old mulch in the burlap sacks, turning over the soil, planting. I relish the wide, open space of the pasture, the adventure of living with the day, just whiling it away. I can stand tall in the pasture because the terrain invites me to, or I can lie down on the spine of the ridge and rub backbones with its massive frame, a skeleton from somewhere way back, very long ago. The hollow shows me the yin and yang of its life, and, in so doing, opens me to mine.

Summer

VIEW FROM THE CURB

Red bricks
Chipped bricks
Pebbles in between
Ants running 'round them
Carry white things

Hitching post
Clank clank
Curb for a chair
Manhole
Streetlight
Dank summer air

Persimmon trees
Flower urns
Screens on the porch
Driveway
Roller skates
Clickety-clack
Thump thump

Stone wall
Orchard wall
Loretto Home side
Bond Street
Summit Street
Best of all
Prospect Street
Home

EIGHT   THE FIRST ROSE OF SUMMER

"Mrs. King, is Jean Ellen there with you?" calls Mrs. Springman across the backyard from her rose garden.

Mom pauses from hanging up Pop's shirt on the clothesline. "No, she's out playing in front of the house."

"Tell her I have my first two rose buds!"

"I'll go find her!" Mom drops my Father's shirt back in the clothes basket and comes looking for me.

"Jean Ellen!" I hear Mom calling as I play on the curb out front. "Oh, there you are," she says, out of breath as she rushes around the side of the house. "Mrs. Springman says to come on over to see her roses. They're budding!"

Sitting sideways on the low rock wall of her garden, sun-bonneted and bent, Elizabeth Springman tends her terraced rose garden that covers the entire length of her backyard facing the Mississippi River. Her floppy straw hat protects the skin of her soft, welcoming face in this treeless spot of the yard, but not her bare hands that reflect the soil she works. Her untied apron strings reveal the bulging pockets of her housedress stuffed with garden tools.

"Here they are!" she triumphantly calls out to us as we hurry along the stone pathway, the Springman dog, Tippy, barking to greet us. Proudly, she displays two red buds cupped between her fingers.

"Oh," I murmur, peering down at them. "They're little-er than me."

Mrs. Springman laughs. "Yes, Jean Ellen, they are certainly smaller than you. These are only the buds, you see, but in a week or so, they'll come to full bloom."

"Can I take one home?" I ask Mom, wanting to keep track of it on the doorway alongside my measurements.

"Goodness gracious, no, honey! You'd kill it if you did that!" Then Mom tells our neighbor how I've been measuring myself every single day to keep up with her roses.

"That's a good girl, Jean Ellen," Mrs. Springman replies, her tone becoming serious. "You just keep measuring your growth as you've been doing, but we have to keep the buds on the vine. They need their mother's nourishment, plus the soil and sun and me to keep them watered. Otherwise, they'd never grow. Flowers are a lot like people," she adds, her voice trailing off. I nod, not quite understanding, but liking the sound of it anyway.

"You always have such nice things to say," Mom tells her thoughtful neighbor, admiringly. "There's so much truth to it."

It wasn't long before Mom was bending low to tenderly cup the face of a bright red rose in her hand. "Oh! Isn't it just beautiful!" she exclaims, her voice catching in her throat with emotion. "The first rose of summer! There's nothing like the deep red of a rose, is there, Mrs. Springman? And look how perfectly it's shaped."

Our neighbor beams with pleasure, seeing Mom's. "I always say, when the American Beauties come into bloom, everything's right with the world." Proudly, she surveys her garden. "There'll be others, too, you know, not just the Beauties. Down towards the hollow will be yellows—my favorites—and along the wall, pinks, then up at the top near the house, whites."

Mom shakes her head in amazement. "All the hard work you put into it, Mrs. Springman, and it sure shows! I wish my flowerbed looked half as good as your rose garden."

"Nonsense, Mrs. King. Yours do just fine."

"No, nothing can compare with your rose garden," my Mother insists. "Everyone on Prospect Street knows that!"

"Joe thinks it's the rock levels that make the garden specially attractive," our neighbor modestly replies, "and the way it faces the Mississippi."

"Just like a man!" my Mother scoffs. "They haven't an inkling of how hard a woman works! A garden like this just doesn't come up on its own." Mrs. Springman looks at a loss for words, so I give her apron a tug.

"Can I smell it?" I ask.

"Goodness gracious!" she exclaims, as if seeing me for the first time. "You've been so quiet, Jean Ellen, I forgot you were here! And you've been waiting so long to see the first rose!" Her face is flushed now, like the rose, as she bends low and coddles me to her side. "And here your Mother and I've been gabbing away…" her voice trails off as she chuckles to herself. "Here, Jean Ellen," she whispers, bending the stem just so the flower is level with my nose. "Now just smell that. It's like perfume." I lean into the velvety petals, and sniff.

"Mmm," I murmur, and run my tongue along my lips.

"Smells good enough to eat, doesn't it?" Mom laughs with pleasure, and I hope she's thinking about making a rose pie for supper, or rose ice cream in our maker like she does with strawberries. Then Mrs. Springman does the most incredible thing. She takes a paring knife out of her pocket, cuts the rose off the vine, and holds it out to me.

"Mrs. Springman, you shouldn't!" Mom protests, but our neighbor ignores her, planting the stem firmly in my hands.

"Here, Jean Ellen, put it in water as soon as you get home. It's yours for as long as it lasts. Someday, when you're full grown, you'll be just as pretty as that rose, and smell just as sweet, too." She chuckles at that last comment.

"I'm afraid there won't be any smell left in that poor flower by the time we reach the house," Mom laughs as we head up the pathway, my nose buried in the petals. "What do you say to Mrs. Springman?"

"Thank you!" I holler over my shoulder, noting that I somehow feel taller than when we first entered the garden.

NINE   INS AND OUTS OF THE NEIGHBORHOOD

Aside from a weekend visit to our parents' friends, the Flynn's, in Franklin, Illinois, or a drive to Pershing Avenue in St. Louis, Missouri, to see Auntie Barb and Uncle Virg, my sister, Barb, and I stay close to hearth and neighborhood. In fact, we probably spend as much time in our neighbors' homes as we do in our own.

We know every inch inside every house on Prospect Street, we play in them so often. We love to go to the Reasoner's where Rufus (a.k.a. Curtis) and Bobby Herrick live during the summers. Their sisters, Anna Belle and Mary, have lush canopy beds that they let us flop around on, or sometimes we just lie quietly and imagine ourselves in a Southern mansion like where their mother came from.

We know Elizabeth and Joe Springman's house like our own because we play with their daughter, JoAnn. Some nights we camp out in tents behind Jimmy Turner's, or, if it rains, sleep upstairs in his family's garage.

Down the street from us on the opposite side, Cora Hutchinson keeps a snake in a large glass aquarium. Cora's mother, Mrs. Wuerker, always wears a choker centered by an old-fashioned brooch. She has a rasping voice, which I mistakenly think is because the choker is too tight. I haven't considered that she is in her nineties.

Mrs. Wuerker, neighbor, and E. J. Morrissey

At the opposite end of Prospect Street, we visit Mrs. Brown, the seamstress who, yes, lives in a brown house across from the Loretto Home, a boarding house for working women. Mrs. Brown is deaf. For this reason, she is the most enthusiastic customer of *Prospect's Newest News,* our neighborhood newspaper. When she speaks, her voice comes from somewhere way back in her throat, making it sound like the echoes we make inside caves on the Mississippi River bluffs. And when she laughs, she sucks the sound inward so hard that I fear she might gag.

Our many-times-removed cousin, Mame Scott, lives in the Loretto Home across from Mrs. Brown. Cousin Mame deserves the world's record for consistently achieving the opposite of her intended goal. When Mom sends us to visit her, Cousin Mame chases us away because she gushes all over us with kisses, and, to make matters worse, she smells like mothballs, so we call her, appropriately, "Mothballs." We also have a name for one of the Klunk sisters who live four doors down from us. Every time Miss Klunk walks past our house, we see her wearing white gloves, so we call her "Mittens."

The best house of all, though, is right next door, the Kitzmiller's. "Kitzie's" is the most outrageous neighbor anyone could ask for. When I grow up, I want to write a story about them, and call it "The Millers" so I don't give them away.

TEN   AH-CHOO!

You know how it is with grownups. Sometimes they ask the silliest questions. Like when they ask you what your name is when they know darn good and well what it is.

One day Mom sent me over to my cousin Paul's house with our sick canary. "Paul says he'll take care of Deidesheimer for me—I just can't do it," she tells me, handing me a bag with the bird inside. "Don't dilly-dally along the way, Jean Ellen. Paul's expecting you." I peer inside the bag and see our poor canary lying very still, but breathing.

So I scamper over to Paul's, carrying the bag containing the ailing bird as carefully as a five-year-old can. When I get to his house, he's working in the yard. Seeing me, he gets to his feet, and with a big grin on his face, says, "Hello there! What's your name, little girl?"

"Ah-choo!" I emphatically reply. My cousin looks at me, surprised, as if it wasn't the answer he was expecting.

"What did you say?" he asks, laughing.

"Ah-choo," I repeat. Paul Morrissey's face is one big question mark, but I can tell he knows that I mean what I say. So he glances at the bag, changing the subject.

"I see you brought your Mom's sick canary over." Gently, he takes the bag from me and looks inside. After a few moments, he says, "C'mon in and we'll see what we can do for your bird."

But when we get inside the house, Paul asks me to wait in the hallway as he goes into the kitchen, and I hear him dialing the phone.

"Hi, Annette. Jean Ellen's here with the canary. Yep, I'll take care of it for you. No, it's no trouble. It's never easy to put a pet to sleep. So don't worry. There's something else that's kind of funny, though. I asked Jean Ellen, 'What's your name, little girl?'—you know how we do with kids—and she flat out said, 'Ah-choo!'"

Mom's excited voice carries clear over the wire. "'Ah-choo'? Where on earth did she pick that up?"

"Darned if I know. Couldn't believe my ears, so I asked her again, just to be sure, but she still insisted that her name was 'Ah-choo.' Annette, I don't think your daughter knows what her real name is!"

"For goodness sake!" Mom replies, bewildered. The silence on the line tells me she's trying to figure it out. Soon she says, "Well, Jean Ellen does sneeze a lot. She plays outdoors as much as in and is always up in Springman's garden smelling the roses. Mrs. Springman says she's afraid someday a bee is going to sting her right on the nose! And my nephew, Virg, has to have his non-allergic pillow when he comes over here to spend the night. So maybe allergies run in the family. But I don't know why in heaven's name Jean Ellen would call herself 'Ah-choo'."

My cousin laughs. "Well, you never know about kids, or where they pick things up. Not that we didn't do the same, of course! Anyway, your canary's here and I'll take care of it, like I said."

"Thank you, Paul. I just couldn't put Deidesheimer to sleep myself."

My Mom's crazy about birds and likes taking care of them. Every night, she covers the cage with a dish towel and removes it first thing in the morning. Cleaning the cage is as important to her as any household chore. We always have a caged bird near a window, but canaries are her favorite 'cause she loves when they sing. That's why she talks to her bird in soft, whistling chirps—trying to get it to sing—and the bird cocks its head and peeps back.

Paul hangs up the phone and calls me into the kitchen. "Let's see what we can do for your bird," he says, taking it out of the bag.

Slowly, he opens the back door to the woods, and before I can ask, "What's ya gonna do, Paul?" he gently tosses Deidesheimer into the air. Then I see it take flight into the trees, and Paul grins from ear to ear.

"Just hope a cat doesn't get it," he murmurs. "Don't tell your Mother what I just did, Jean Ellen."

"Okay, Paul!" and I head for the door, happy to see Deidesheimer fly to the woods, his home in the great outdoors.

"Go straight home, and tell your folks hello," he calls after me.

I wave good-bye, 'cause by now, I'm out the door and skipping up the street toward home.

Paul Morrissey, my cousin and Ann's dad

That night, when Mom is tucking me under the covers, she says she's relieved that Paul took care of the bird. I keep my promise to him, not saying a word, because I'm thinking Paul's just like Mom— he couldn't put the bird to sleep either. Anyhow, I bet Deideshimer is

43

sitting on a branch right now, or making a nest high up in a tree where a cat can't get him. That would make Mom happy. That's how come she hates those sneaky cats—they go after birds.

I'm about to fall asleep, when Mom asks, "Jean Ellen, when you were over there today, what did you tell Paul your name was?"

"Ah-choo."

"Why on earth did you tell him that?"

"'Cause."

"Because why? You know your name's Jean Ellen."

Some time later, I'm sitting on Grandpa's lap while he reads to me, and Mom comes in, dusting around the room. Suddenly, I sneeze—once, twice, three times—and Grandpa looks at me and exclaims—with gusto—"Ah-choo!"

ELEVEN   PLAY BALL!

I hear the crack of the bat and I'm off and running down the first base line just like my idol, Stan Musial. Grazing the bag with my foot, I round first and head toward second digging my heels into the footprints of Red Schoendiest. Glaring ballpark lights beat down on me, but even more, the distance between bases feels as long as the drive from Alton to St. Louis. Ruts from players' cleats covering the infield trip me up, but I race on with all the might my five years can muster. Rounding second, I run to third and slide into the bag, Enos Slaughter style. Getting up, I pause just long enough to dust myself off, then gallop on down the third base line for home.

"Hey, kiddo!" my Father hollers through cupped hands as I cross the plate. "Had enough?" I trot towards him as he stands there in the front row seats of the stadium and pull up, resting my hands on my waist to catch my breath like any home run hitter would do. With my forefinger, I wipe the sweat off my forehead and shake it off. Then I raise my arms and my Father lifts me back into the stands.

"The diamond looks a lot smaller from over here, doesn't it, Jean Ellen?" he laughs, putting me down. "But you ran those bases just like a pro." He turns to my uncle. "Wouldn't you say so, Mart?"

Uncle Mart King nods his assent. "The Redbirds'll be signing her up before the season's over," he replies, flipping the ashes from his cigarette, and I giggle, happy that he thinks me a Cardinal. I look around at the fans filing out of the stadium. The game's over, and they're elated that the St. Louis Cardinals just beat the Brooklyn Dodgers, 6-1. It's the summer of 1943, and we're at Sportsman's Park in North St. Louis, home of the National League Cardinals and American League Browns.

"Can we go get autographs?" Barb wants to know.

"Don't see why not," Pop tells her, and we scurry out to the aisle. "Hold on, girls," he calls after us. "We've got plenty of time. The players have to shower after the game, you know. Wait here 'til the crowd thins. Jean Ellen, let me see how you did with that score card." I meander on back to him and pull out the rumpled card from my jeans pocket. My Father settles down in the seat and tilts back his hat, examining my card. This is the first baseball season that he's taught me how to keep score.

"Let's see," he says, a mischievous grin playing on his face—my Father loves teasing me. "We have one Cracker Jack, two hot dogs with mustard, three Coca-Colas, and about four Double Bubble gums." I try to snatch the card from him, but he hides it at his side, laughing. I scoot onto his lap now as he looks again at the card, this time commenting to himself, "Um-hum, yeah, that's right, you even marked the steal. But where's the rest of the team?" He holds the card out to me pointing to the blank boxes.

"She'll be taking over Caray's job before you know it," Uncle Mart goes on, but I know he's probably joking 'cause Mom says no one can broadcast the game like Harry Caray, the Cardinals' sports announcer. She says you can tell by the tone in Caray's voice if the Redbirds are winning or losing.

I look down sheepishly at the score card because I had kept only my heroes' scores. "Now, can you tell me what Musial did in the seventh inning?" Pop asks me.

"Hit a homer!" I immediately reply without looking at the card.

"No, kiddo," he laughs, "look what you marked on the card, not what you think he did." I peer close and come up with...

"Flied out to center."

"Looks like he did it the same time you were gulping down that hot dog," he teases again, pointing at the mustard smear in the box. The grownups chuckle as he hands me the score card.

By now, the stands have all but emptied out. "Can we go now?" Barb asks. Pop looks around the stadium.

"All right, girls, but don't get too far ahead of us."

The crowd waiting outside the Cardinal locker room is thick as Barb and I begin inching our way to the front. All of a sudden, everyone cheers, so we know the players are coming out. Barb grabs my hand, pulling me on, but we get stuck in the thick of the crowd. Peering around someone's elbow, I get a glimpse of the players as one by one they amble out. I'm not even sure who I'm looking at 'cause the players don't look at all like when they're on the field, all dressed up in suits and ties looking much bigger close up and handsomer. Amicably, they sign autographs on baseballs, score cards, gloves, whatever fans hand them.

When Stan the Man Musial appears, the crowd goes wild, and I get shoved out to the edge, losing my sister. Suddenly, the crowd breaks up as some take off, chasing him. I see Musial heading for the front gate of the stadium and I take off, too, crawling under the turnstile just seconds ahead of Stan the Man. But he's as fast off the field as on 'cause before I know it he's crossing the street and disappearing into the parking lot. If he hadn't stopped to find his keys, I'd have lost him.

"Hey, Stan," I breathlessly call out to him, "would you sign this for me?" And I hold up the ball Pop gave me just for the occasion. Stan the Man Musial turns around and looks at me with that swanky smile of his, takes out a pen and signs the ball. I stare at his name and whisper "Wow!" just as I feel his hand brush the top of my head. Then he's in the car and I race back across the street where everyone's waiting.

"D'ya get it?" Barb asks, but I'm too excited to even answer.

"She sure did!" Pop proudly exclaims, taking the ball out of my hand, examining the autograph.

"Who'd you get?" I ask Barb.

"Slaughter!" and she holds up her score card for me to see the player's scrawl.

My Father hands the ball to Uncle Mart who turns it around and around in his hand and I'm getting antsy thinking he'll wear off the ink. "Bet you'll hit a homer every time you play with this one," he remarks. Vehemently, I nod in agreement. Already I can see the ball sailing past the streetlight on Prospect Street and over the wall into the Loretto Home orchard. Harry Caray's voice rings in my ears, "It *might* be, it *could* be, it *is* a home run!"

Although my family are Cardinal fans, I like watching the Browns play, too, although most years they rank in "the cellar," meaning last place. With the Browns, I'm so used to them losing that I don't even keep a scorecard, just have fun watching the game. Their star pitcher, Satchel Paige, winds up three, four, five times, then hurls the ball to batters who hit clear out of the ballpark. So there's lots of homers, though they're not by the home team. But the best part is a guy in the stands, who everyone calls "Wringy" 'cause he imitates Satchel's wind up until I swear his arm's going to fall right off, all the while screeching like a rusty wheel at the top of his lungs. He's got a burr haircut that stands straight on end, and glasses tied by a string to the back of his head to keep them from falling off when he winds. No matter how hot the weather, "Wringy" always wears a windbreaker.

Another thing I like about going to the Browns' games, the vendors never seem to stop yelling.

Popcorn here! Frrresh popcorn!
Hot dogs! Get your red...hot...dogs, here!
Ice cream! Soda pop! Ice cream, soda pop, here!
Peanuts! Cracker Jack! Peanuts! Cracker Jack!
Coooca Cola! Ice cold Coke, here!

But the best part about baseball is playing it back home on Prospect Street. Baseball and Summer are synonymous in our neighborhood. Our diamond is in the street at the top of Bond: first base, the lamp post on the corner; second base, a rock in the center of the street; third base, the hitching post in front of our house; and home plate, the manhole in the center at Prospect and Bond. One thing you don't want to do, though, is hit a line drive down the sewer by the curb—the rule is that whoever does that has to go down the smelly ol' sewer after it.

My Father James Joseph (Jimmie) King

TWELVE   JAMES JOSEPH KING

Jimmie King had a dance in his step and wit on his tongue, a head full of curls and charm that would go a long way with Antoinette (Annie) Morrissey and her father, E. J. Morrissey. An enterprising young man, Jimmie had dropped out of school before finishing eighth grade, and commuted by bus to Edwardsville, Illinois, where he obtained a job in a shoe store. No wonder his ad in the *Alton Evening Telegraph* at age 20 had caught her father's eye.

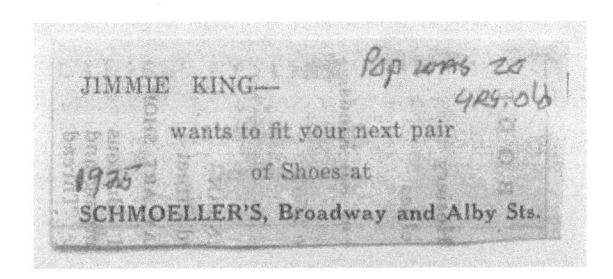

JIMMIE KING—
wants to fit your next pair
of Shoes at
SCHMOELLER'S, Broadway and Alby Sts.

51

Mr. Morrissey needed an extra man in the store, and he liked a man eager and confident enough to sell himself in the city's newspaper. Jimmie's gentle voice on the phone had not escaped Annie when she called him to come in for an interview either.

So Jimmie had two things going for him when he appeared at Morrissey Brothers Shoes one morning: the boss and his daughter. He would later say that he was a shoe-in to get the job—laughing at his own joke.

Hearing someone whistling at the store entrance, Annie looked up from her typewriter. A tall, lean man closed the door and stepped inside. Hat in hand, he approached her desk, grinning and winning.

"Morning," he said, smiling down at her, "I'm Jimmie King. I have an appointment with Mr. Morrissey at 10:00 o'clock."

"Nice to meet you," Annie replied, removing paper from her typewriter. "Please have a seat. Dad's in the back. I'll tell him you're here."

Beneath a visor and surrounded by ledgers, E. J. Morrissey rose from his desk as Annie entered his office. "Jimmie King is here," was all Annie could say, turning quickly away so her Father could not see the red in her burning cheeks that she was certain was there. Checking his stopwatch, Morrissey nodded in approval, pleased that the twenty-year-old King had arrived on time, and strode through the office gate to meet him.

Jimmie had sales experience having been employed by Schmoeller's Shoes up Broadway hill from Morrissey's. He liked the retail business; his congenial personality worked well for him in that role. Morrissey Brothers Shoes was the number one shoe retailer in town, he knew, and its location on West Third Street in the downtown business district, the heart of the city, attracted him.

Since early days, the business was called Morrissey Brothers Shoes, founded by E. J. and his brothers, Will and John. Today, E. J. and a son, Edmund, carried on the business. Jimmie knew that working at Morrissey's would be challenging—a better-paying job demanded it, but he couldn't help smiling just at the thought of working there. It was personal, too, for in his heart, he knew he wanted to work further away from his home on Broadway that was located only three doors from Schmoeller's. And, he'd admit only to himself, hadn't he seen that attractive Annie Morrissey at a restaurant several weeks ago? She seemed the life of the party, though he couldn't catch her eye.

The interview went well, and on the following Monday, Jimmie King began his first day working as a salesman at Morrissey Brothers Shoes.

The third oldest of six children in a close-knit, Irish family, Jimmie outshone his siblings socially. "My family's a strange lot," he later remarked to Annie. His father was a glass blower at Illinois Glass, his two brothers worked for a printing company, one sister was employed at St. Joseph's Hospital and another at city hall in neighboring Edwardsville. All the men, except Jimmie, walked to work, which prompted Annie to exclaim, "Imagine! Grown men and they can't even drive a car!" But Jimmie was outgoing and sensitive, she thought. And he drove a car!

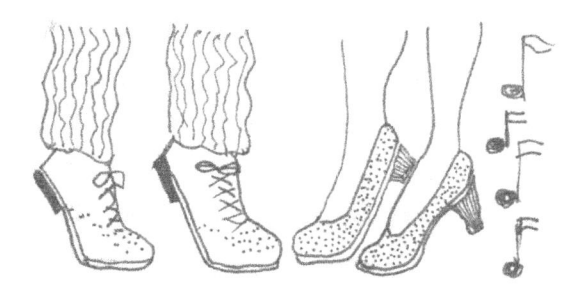

That he had a bounce to his step, a whistle on his lips, and wit on the ready, made it easy for Annie to fall for him. King enjoyed sports and was a St. Louis Cardinal baseball fan, but his first love was music. Francis Kramer, who owned Kramer Music Store across Broadway from the King's home, remarked, "That kid can hear a tune only once and he's got it." And it was true. Listening to the radio program, "Name That Tune," Jimmie knew the title of a song

53

on the first note. But neither he nor Kramer could persuade the Kings to give their son piano lessons. They were afraid that taking music lessons would "make him effeminate." So Jimmie whistled the songs he heard, and, in so doing, became his own musical instrument.

One of them eggs is . . .

THIRTEEN SUNDAY MORNINGS

Sunday mornings at Springman's is not at all like at our house, I soon discover. For one thing, Mrs. Springman serves breakfast at the right time—all morning long. Soon as someone comes home from Mass, they get to eat. After all, Joe-Boy says, they've been fasting since midnight for Holy Communion. Mrs. Springman goes to early Mass at the Cathedral just so she can fix breakfast for her family—Canadian bacon breakfast.

After everyone's eaten and the dishes are done, Mr. and Mrs. Springman read the St. Louis Post-Dispatch Sunday paper in their living room, the papers strewn all over the wrap-around flowered divan, as they exchange reading sections. JoAnn and her older sisters, Mary Louise and Dolores, take to the front parlor where, from their grand piano, they sing songs of light opera, like Indian Love Call and The Student Prince. I sit in a chair and listen. It's like having the Forest Park Muny Opera right here in their parlor. JoAnn's voice is as pretty as her mother's roses. Her brothers, Eugene, Jerome, Gerald, Ed, and Joe-Boy, all go sit on their screened-in front porch for a while, and eventually just go for a Sunday morning drive.

At our house, we have our big meal at noon, which means we have to wait 'til lunch time to eat breakfast. Before I figured out how to eat Canadian bacon and watch Mrs. Springman's roses from her kitchen on Sunday mornings, I drove Mom crazy pestering her and Ida Henretti, our housekeeper, for tidbits to tide me over until our Sunday company arrived.

Uncle Gene Morrissey and his daughter, Jean Louise, always stop by on their way to and from Mass, and priests from the parish come after the last Mass. We all eat together in the dining room, and I always know when the meal's almost over 'cause Uncle Gene dumps all the left-overs into a blue vegetable bowl and finishes them up.

Then everyone's gone before you know it: Dad to the Cardinal ballgame in St. Louis, Uncle Gene and Jean Louise back to their house on Summit Street, the priests to their rectory, Gramps to his back room, and Barbara and I go outside to chase around the backyard with our dog, Wiggles. Mom and Idy are left with the dishes, and about an hour or so later, I hear Idy go klump, klump, klump down the back porch steps in her big, black Oxfords to her home three doors down the street from ours.

St. Louis Cardinal baseball fans pose at old Clark Bridge:
(l to r) Ed Barrett, Uncle Mart King, Clem Goeken, my Father
Jimmie King, Great Uncle Mike Fitzgerald

Mom says the priests' invitation to our house on Sundays is a carry-over from when she was a little girl, and that even back then my Uncle Gene ate everything left in sight. I bet that's how come he still gets away with it. But the real wonder, Mom says, is that the priests still come at all the way my uncles and aunt carried on at the table, not to mention some of the dumb things Idy did.

The Sunday morning breakfast, today called brunch, was held at the very same table in our dining room as now and Grandpa Morrissey sat at the head, just like he does with us. On those mornings, though, he faced Monsignor Spalding, his pastor and friend, who sat at the foot, where my Father sits now. To the pastor's right was his young Irish assistant, Father Thomas J. O'Neill, and to his left, my grandmother, Barbara, where Mom now sits, within easy reach of the kitchen to assist Idy with the food. Sandwiched between the church representatives and adults were my Mother, her three brothers and sister: Jim, Ed, Gene, and Barbara.

My Grandparents E. J. Morrissey and
Barbara Blake Morrissey

Having said grace, Monsignor Spalding congenially opened the conversation, directing it to Grandpa. "Ed," he began, placing his napkin on his lap, "on my way up Prospect Street this morning, I was

57

reflecting upon the Almighty's benevolence in providing you and Barbara with such a fine family." The pastor gestured with outstretched hands, like the Good Shepherd he emulated, toward his flock of little Morrisseys sitting silently to both sides of him. "Indeed, I know many a parishioner who would give their right arm to propagate such exemplar children."

"Thank you, Monsignor," Grandpa responded, modestly. "Nonetheless, I propose that most families in the parish are equally as proud of their own."

"Perhaps, my friend, but I must say, albeit there may be a slight bias in my doing so, that if I had fathered a family, I would have modeled them much like your own." Again, the pastor smiled upon the five little Morrisseys, sitting awkwardly, subdued.

Grandpa leaned forward, and with a twinkle in his eyes, said, "Indeed, I am grateful for the compliment, Monsignor, but I think I'll keep all five!"

The adults laughed, and Monsignor Spalding leaned back in his chair, pleasurably. He looked forward to this time on Sundays after the hectic Mass schedule when he could relax in the company of his friend and devout parishioner, E. J. Morrissey. Reaching for the coffee cup Idy had just filled, he drank and patted his lips. "Ahhh," he sighed, "there's nothing like a good cup of Miss Henretti's coffee to top off the morning." Idy glanced at him sidelong, rolled her eyes, and returned to the kitchen where the smell of bacon and eggs slowly permeated the room. Addressing Jim, the oldest of my uncles, the pastor continued, "Now here is a strapping young fellow who's the model of manners. 'May I pass you the cream, Father? Do you take sugar with your coffee?'" the priest intoned, imitating Jim. The five Morrisseys began to giggle. "Yes," the pastor concluded, oblivious of their reaction, "Father O'Neill and I are indeed fortunate to be in such fine company." He then turned to his assistant. "Don't you agree, Tom?"

Father Thomas J. O'Neill

The young cleric, who had been staring into the tablecloth during his pastor's complimentaries, shot a glance around the table and smiled faintly. "Surely," he responded in his crisp Irish brogue, then quickly reached for his coffee, took a gulp, and returned to his contemplation of the tablecloth.

"Yes, well," the pastor muttered, embarrassed and confounded by his assistant's unusual lack of conversation. Before this moment, O'Neill was as talkative and engaging a man that Spalding had ever met, having the Irish "gift of gab" always at hand. "Only yesterday," Spalding continued, "Father O'Neill was telling me how much he looked forward to these Sundays with the Morrisseys."

Just then, Idy came into the dining room carrying a platter piled high with fried eggs and plunked it down in the center of the table. The children, relieved of the conversation, grabbed their forks as if preparing for battle. But just as Idy was returning to the kitchen, she looked over her shoulder and matter-of-factly declared, "*One* of them eggs is *bad*!" Forks hung in the balance, and a gasp traveled around the table as all eyes fixed upon the suspect platter of eggs.

"I suppose none of us will be the worse for it," Grandpa scowled, saving the moment.

"Sure'n those who are starvin' fare far worse," offered Father O'Neill, the first sentence he had spoken since coming to the table.

Minutes passed as the family partook of the eggs, cautiously, at first, before conversation ensued and the pastor, encouraged by his cleric's comment, tried again to elicit conversation from him.

"The Cathedral is Father O'Neill's first parish assignment since his mission up in Pana," Spalding said. "And, of course, as you all know, he also teaches religion classes in our school. Isn't that so, Tom?" Father O'Neill replied with a nod, pointing to his filled mouth to indicate it was impossible for him to speak. "And how is that going?" Spalding pressed on.

O'Neill looked nervously around the table like a man doomed to the scaffold. He swallowed hard, and sat back in his chair, resigned. "'Tis well, Father," he replied, almost in a whisper.

"Are any of Ed's children in your classes?" the pastor eagerly asked, hoping to finally engage Father O'Neill in conversation.

"Yes, Monsignor," O'Neill replied. He folded his hands on his lap now and stared blankly again at the tablecloth.

"How many? One? Two?"

Father O'Neill held up his hand, his fingers pointed heavenward.

"Five!" the pastor exclaimed. "*All* five?" Hearing this, he put down his fork and rested his elbows on the table, savoring the moment. Posing his fingers in the shape of the Cathedral steeple, he smiled upon each child. "All well-behaved, I'm sure!"

"Well-behaved?" Father O'Neill blurted out, incredulously. "In the name of Holy Mary, Father, 'tis not like any behavior I've ever encountered!" Grandpa's head jerked up, and Grandma knew without looking that her children were staring innocently at the ceiling. "But we were all kids once," the young cleric went on, apologetically, "so 'tis quite understandable that at times in the classroom, when a child would rather be out playin'…"

Someone giggled.

"Edmund!" Grandpa reprimanded, "Father O'Neill is speaking."

"Sorry, Father."

"You were saying, Father O'Neill?" E. J. pressed on, his curiosity intensifying.

The priest moved uncomfortably in his chair and looked to Grandma in desperation, but she, too, was fixated on the tablecloth. "I j-j-just meant," he stammered, "that I can always count on the Morrissey children to liven up me classes a bit. Quick minds, you know, an'…well…they're always…umm…full of…the ol' Nick, so to speak."

"The children have their mother's keen mind, to be sure," Grandpa said, appreciably, "but what exactly do you mean by 'the ol' Nick', Father?"

"He means like in e-a-r-s!" Barbara blurted out.

"Spelled E-u-g-e-n-e!" Ed laughed, pointing to his brother.

"Barbara, Edmund! I'll have no such outbursts at this table!" Grandpa admonished them. But Grandma, looking over at her youngest child who was now squirming in his chair, knew the tide was in, and her children were racing toward the beach.

"Gene can wiggle his ears for ten whole counts without stopping!" Nina excitedly went on, her face aglow with mischief at the thought. "Tommy Tracy had to stand in the corner because he couldn't stop laughing!" More giggles.

"Eugene, my boy, do you…wiggle…your ears during class?" Grandpa asked, aghast.

Gene looked quickly around the table, hung his head, and murmured, "Yes, Dad." The children laughed outright and their mother stifled hers in her napkin.

"Instead of attending to your studies?"

"Only sometimes, Dad. I only wiggle 'em sometimes."

"But, my boy! You are not in school to entertain your classmates! Am I to understand that you are misbehaving in class?" Grandpa turned to Father O'Neill for an answer, but the unresponsive cleric only sat there, doomed to failure.

"Oh, but he looks so *funny*, Dad!" Barbara burst out again, gleefully pounding both fists on the table. "You should just see him! Oh, please, Dad, let Gene wiggle 'em now!"

Before Grandpa could respond, all eyes focused upon Gene Morrissey's elf-like ears, glowing red now with excitement, his eyes dancing with mischief. Tuned to his audience, he looked first at his Dad and wiggled one ear, then at his Mother and wiggled the other, and finally eyed each individual around the entire table, wiggling them both. The table broke up laughing, turning the sedate Sunday brunch into pandemonium. Only Gene Morrissey sat perfectly still, wiggling his ears for all they were worth without moving a single feature on his impish Irish face.

Uncle Gene "Wigglin' Ears" Morrissey

Grandfather Edmund (E. J.) Morrissey

FOURTEEN RITUALS

> "One, two, buckle my shoe
> Three, four, shut the door..."

Singsonging, I sit on the curb in front of our house, absently scraping pebbles out from between the bricks on the street with a stick. Every now and then, I glance up the street, but seeing no one, resume singsonging.

> "Five, six, pick up sticks
> Seven, eight, lay them straight..."

"Here he comes!" Mom calls out from the porch. Jumping up, I stand tiptoe on the curb, straining to see. Sure enough, the familiar solitary figure appears at the top of Prospect Street hill. Excitedly, I begin clanking the ring against the hitching post announcing his coming like joy bells at the Cathedral on Easter morning. Then I dash to the sidewalk to meet him, but Mom cuts me short. "Wait'll he crosses the street, Jean Ellen, then you can go." So for the next few minutes, Mom and I watch expectantly as Grandpa Morrissey walks home from his visit to church.

Gramps has his routine. Hands clasped behind his back, head bowed in thought, he walks alongside the orchard wall on the Loretto Home side of our street. A passing car may cause him to raise his head, but only long enough to acknowledge the driver with a slight wave of the hand and then return to his thoughts that mirror his long, deliberate stride.

The closer he comes, the bigger he gets, as does my eagerness to meet him. I watch for his next move, which occurs as timely as the setting sun. From inside his vest, he takes out his pocket watch, pauses to read it, returns it, and continues walking. I know precisely the point where he'll cross the street—always at Springman's—my signal to run.

He steps off the curb into the street, and I'm off like a shot.

Looking up, he feigns surprise upon seeing me, then cautions me to "stay on the curb" before he reaches my side. Then hand in hand, we walk together back to the house.

As we walk up the driveway, Mom comes down the porch steps to greet us. "Hello, Dad. Looks like you have a helper with you today."

"Yes, my girl," he replies. "I have a fine little helper with me every day, indeed." He lets go of my hand now, and peers down at me. "I don't know how I'd ever get across Prospect Street without her," and for some reason, they both laugh.

Once inside, Grandpa tucks a copy of the *Alton Evening Telegraph* under his arm and heads for the back room, *his* room, and I trail along behind. Setting the newspaper on his pipe-stand, he replaces his suit coat with a smoking jacket from which he removes his tobacco pouch, and settles into his armchair. Placing the paper in his lap, he puts on his reading visor, but I know he'll never get to reading the paper.

  Picking up his pipe from the stand, he knocks out the dank ashes and sprinkles in fresh tobacco with his index finger, while I, leaning against the arm of his chair, take in the sweet aroma. Carefully, he folds up the pouch and returns it to his jacket. For the next few minutes, he ceremoniously packs the tobacco in the bowl with his thumb, periodically inspecting it under his bifocals. Satisfied, he deftly strikes a match against the side of the stand, careful to shield the flame as he brings it to the bowl. Then, in short, sporadic puffs, with eyes focused steadily upon the tobacco, he lights it.

  Now Grandpa draws on the pipe, and the deeper he draws, the deeper his cheeks billow in and out, like the goldfish in Uncle Ed's aquarium, I'm thinking. Entranced by the spectacle, I mimic him, forcing my cheeks in and out. At length, he suspends the ritual and rests his head back on the chair, reflectively drawing on the pipe that hangs from his mouth, making soft "lapping" sounds as he draws. Absently, he glances at the paper lying conspicuously on his lap, holds it up just long enough to scan the headlines, then places it back down, the pleasure of smoking the pipe consuming him, and I, too, rest my chin in my hands, enjoying the sweet, delectable aroma. Tiny smoke rings escape him that quickly form into larger ones. Lazily, they float about the room, slowly changing shape like clouds, then disappear into the light of late afternoon.

  Suddenly, I sneeze, and he sees me as though for the first time. A smile spreads across his face, and the twinkle in his eyes alerts me to what is coming next—his specialty. So I scamper behind his chair, and wait. Deeply, he draws on the pipe, retaining the smoke in his mouth, places it on the stand, and, with hands cupped at his cheeks, blows the smoke seemingly out his ears. Squealing with delight, I entreat him, "Do it again, Grandpa! Do it again!"

But the commotion brings Mom into the room, announcing that supper is almost on the table, which is her way of calming me down. But I protest. "Better mind your Mother," Gramps tells me, getting out of his chair. "You'll never grow up if you don't eat." Decidedly, he tosses the paper back on the chair, removes his visor and smoking jacket, and heads straightway for the dining room.

"One thing about E. J.," I hear Mom telling our maid, Idy, in the kitchen, "he's got such a good appetite, I can always count on him to get the girls to stop playing and come to the table."

On evenings when Gramps' brother, Will Morrissey, joins him in the back room to listen to the 5 o'clock news on the radio, Gramps changes his routine. He doesn't even take the newspaper back with him, and his visor's nowhere to be seen. He never wears his smoking jacket, and when he lights up his pipe, he stokes it fast without blowing smoke rings. From under the dining room table, I watch, 'cause Mom tells me not to bother Grandpa when he and his brother are trying to listen to the news.

On and on Gabriel Heatter, the news commentator, drones. Pretty soon Uncle Will's eyes close, his head nods, and his chin hits his chest, fast asleep. In a few minutes, Gramps snarls, "Ah, rats!" at the commentator, which rouses Uncle Will.

"What's that you say, Edmund?" he asks, looking around the room, disoriented. Grandpa ignores him, and cups his ear toward the radio, scowling. Moments later, Uncle Will's chin plunks back down on his chest, and before long, the broadcast ends.

"Will!" Grandpa calls to him. "The news is over!" Up my uncle jumps, puts on his hat, and stumbles out of the room to the front door, muttering about the news of the day he did not hear.

Most evenings, though, we play hide-and-seek after supper, with me hiding and Gramps seeking. As soon as the table is cleared, we're off, racing around the dining room until Mom runs in from the kitchen, crying out, "Dad! Watch out for the china!" Our china cabinet stands vulnerably against the wall leading to Gramps' back room. After admonishing me to mind my Mother, he takes his leave into his room.

Some nights, when Uncle Gene and his daughter, Jean Louise, come for supper, Jean Louise and I hide under the dining room table—and tonight, she has crayons.

Grandpa settles in his armchair, engrossed in reading the *Alton Evening Telegraph*. Cautiously, my cousin and I crawl out from under the table and, on all fours, slide over the threshold into his room where, bellying down, we wind like snakes around chairs until we reach our destination—the back of his. Stifling giggles, we stand up and proceed to draw faces on his bald head as he reads. After a minute or so, he starts swatting the air around his head with the paper. "My goodness!" he mutters. "There must be a *fly* in here!" Quickly, we flop to the floor until he resumes reading and then we begin to draw again.

This time, though, he abruptly jumps up from his chair, and we freeze. Rolling up the paper, he heads around the side, swatting the arm of the chair as he comes, muttering, "*Where's* that fly? I *must* get that fly!" Unable to contain ourselves any longer, we jump frantically up and down in full view. "Goodness gracious!" he cries out. "*Look* at the flies I found! *Two* of them!" And he waves the paper in the air as, indeed, we fly out of the room, stumbling on our laughter before he catches us.

At bedtime, Jean Louise, my sister, Barbara, and I often read saints' stories to each other from Mom's Daily Missal, or make up games about our neighbors and their houses, like "Who do you think's the prettiest?" or "Whose house do you like the best?" And most nights, we listen to radio programs.

Monday nights feature *The LEMAC Hour*, a quiz show sponsored by Camel cigarettes. (LEMAC stands for Camel spelled backwards.) Then comes *My Friend, Irma*, a comedy about a wacky gal from Minnesota. Sunday nights host another comedy, *The Great Gildersleeve*, which is based upon the simple premise that every time Gildersleeve opens his closet, its contents come crashing over the radio waves—something we strongly identify with. Sunday night also features characters Jack Benny and Rochester, Amos and Andy, and Kingfish. Finally, *Lorenzo Jones and His Wife, Belle* round out the evening.

But when Mom and Pop tell us it's time to turn out the light, we protest. So what do they do? They paste flourescent galaxies around our ceiling light, creating a skylight in our 1850s home. To see the universe, we have to turn off the light. In their wisdom, they expose us to the splendor of the heavens and get us to turn off the light at the same time.

Autumn

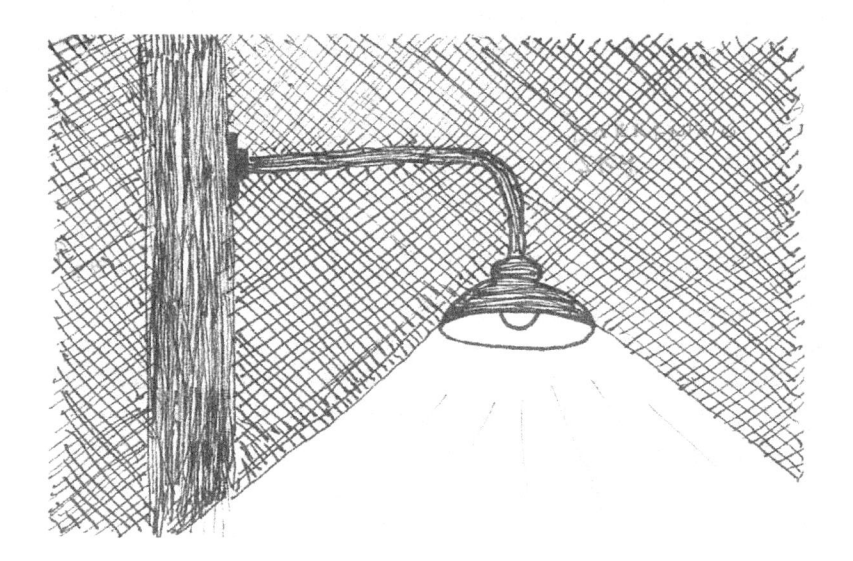

"OLLY OLLY OXEN FREE!"

"Olly Olly Oxen Free!"
I call to my neighborhood chums
Hiding on Prospect Street
In the dim evening light

"Olly Olly Oxen Free!
Olly Olly Oxen Free!"
I chant again, this time adding,
"Hey! Y'all! Come on in!"

But no one stirs

"Olly Olly Oxen Frrreeeee!"
I yell now, annoyed
"Come on home

So we can play another game
Before the streetlight comes on!"

Ghost-like, the players slowly emerge
Around corners, over walls
Spilling into the street
Like Halloween tricksters
Poking each other in jest
Giddy on the cool Autumn air

"Hurry up or the streetlight'll come on!"
I urge once again

All at once they run towards me
Converging over the manhole
In the center of Prospect Street
Where I stand

Quickly, we choose up sides
And into the oncoming night they scatter
Racing against time
Dictated by the threatening lamppost overhead

Breathless, the players crouch
Behind trees, under porches
Wild things smelling the scent of the game

Which is to distract me
Catch me off guard
As I cautiously hunt them down
Before they pounce from their hiding
And race across the manhole
Home

But the streetlight flicks on
Illuminating the street
My chums' groans
Weigh heavy on the air

Slowly, the shadowy figures appear
Reluctant performers upon the stage of
"Olly Olly Oxen Free"

Suddenly, our front door swings open
And Mom cheerfully calls from the porch
"Barbara Blake, Jean Ellen, time to come in now
Streetlight's on!"

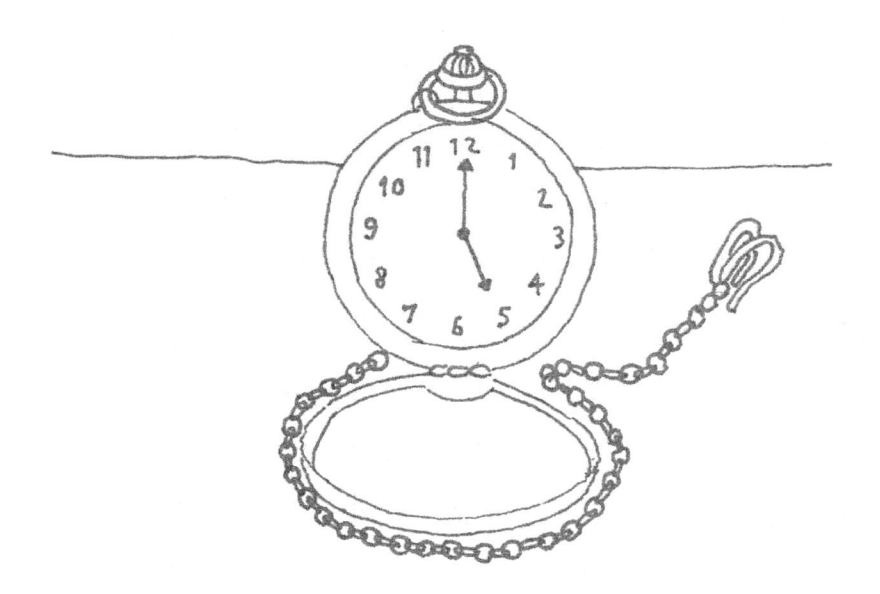

FIFTEEN   A TIMELY LESSON

"Time to come in now, Jean Ellen," Mom calls to me from the front porch.

"But I just started playing!" I holler back as I shoot a glance at the lamppost across the street from our house. When the streetlight comes on, it's our signal to stop playing and come inside.

"I know, honey, but it's getting dark. The days are shorter now that Winter's coming."

It's early evening in late November, the time after supper when my sister and I eke out the last remnants of the day to play before bedtime. Reluctantly, I turn my tricycle into the driveway and circle up to the porch. Across the street, the streetlight appears dull in the approaching dim. In Summer, we play secure in the knowledge that our parents can't call us inside before the light, like clockwork, illuminates the corner of Prospect and Bond streets at 8 o'clock. The streetlight is the cornerstone upon which our world of play depends.

"The light comes on earlier now, Jean Ellen, just like in Wintertime."

"It doesn't even come on in Winter," I stubbornly reply, trying to hold on to my precious play time.

"Sure it does!" Mom laughs. "You just don't see it because you don't go back out to play after supper. In Winter, it's pitch black out here by then." Mom holds the screen door open and we go inside. Flopping on a chair in the front parlor, I gaze out the window at the lamppost, pouting. "You're getting bigger now, honey," Mom says, trying to soothe me. "Soon you'll realize things happen you never noticed before." But I only turn my back to her, which makes her laugh again. "Heavens, Jean Ellen! You can't expect the seasons to stay the same just to suit you!" I look up at her, dismayed. All I know is, I don't get to play outside as long now as I did all Summer, and that makes me grumpy. Then suddenly, I think of Grandpa.

I'm out of the chair and running down the hall to the back room. As usual, I find him sitting in his chair, reading. "Well, well, look who's here!" he greets me as I race into the room. "Come to visit Grandpa, have you?" He sets aside his book and makes room for me in his chair. Eagerly, I climb up beside him. "Have you been playing outside, little girl?"

"Yes, Grandpa, but I had to come in early because the streetlight's already on." Tears fill my eyes.

"There, there," he says, cuddling me. "I'll bet you didn't like that very much, did you!" Vehemently, I shake my head in agreement, my lips quivering. Then he reaches into his vest pocket, pulls out his watch, and flips open the cover. The light from his floor lamp bounces off its glistening face, so Gramps adjusts his reading visor which Mom says protects his eyes from the glare. "See, little girl," he says, pointing to the watch, "it's already getting dark, just like your Mother said. Winter will be here before we know it." Like magic, my pouting lifts, and my mind quickly turns to other things. A question begins to form, and after a few moments, I have it.

"What time is the streetlight on?" I ask, peering into the face of the clock. My grandfather looks away for a moment, considering the question. Then he gazes at me, and I feel the warmth of his smile cover me.

"You want to know what time looks like when the streetlight comes on, is that it, little girl?" he asks. I nod, sensing the clarity of my question in his own. "Well," he says, enthusiastically, "let's see if we can find the number 5 on Grandpa's watch." Slowly, he counts the numbers up to 5, pointing to each as he goes, and I tap my feet in rhythm with his voice. "There!" he declares, pointing to the figure in question, that's what 5 looks like." I peer closer at the numeral and see the streetlight swirling in it. Pointing to myself, I raise five fingers. "Just like me!" I exclaim. "I'm five years old, Grandpa."

"That is correct, little girl, just like you." Instantly, my eagerness to learn to tell time excludes all other reality. "Now, little girl, help Grandpa count the numbers." So together, we count time, Grandpa pointing to the numerals as he names them and me repeating after him, raising my fingers as we go. "Very good!" he exclaims, smiling down at me, approvingly. "Now, let's see if you can count them all by yourself." So I begin tapping my feet again in rhythm with the numbers that spill out of me as easily as melting ice cream on a Summer day. When I exclaim, "Five!" Gramps laughs, amused, and challenges me further. "Let's continue now and count all the way around the clock." So on we go until we reach 10 and I've run out of fingers. Gramps winks and lends me two of his own.

By now, the room has fallen into darkness save for our spot under the floor lamp. Then, like the approaching nighttime, Gramps' final instruction comes. "Listen very carefully, little girl, to what Grandpa tells you, for this is the most important part about telling time." I look up at his wise old face, and wait. "The little hand always points to the hour, and the big hand points to the minutes, and when the big hand is on 12, we call it 'o'clock'. That means the time is right on the hour." I stare at the hands on the clock, imprinting in my mind this timely lesson. Then my grandfather holds the watch directly in front of me. "Now, little girl, tell Grandpa what number the big hand is pointing to."

"12!"

"And the little hand?"

"5!"

In the distance, the clock at the Cathedral begins to strike. Without speaking, Gramps and I hustle out of his chair and down the hall to the front parlor window just in time to see the streetlight come on. It's 5 o'clock in the approaching season of Winter.

SIXTEEN GOOD STOCK

"What's ya doin', Mom?"
"Preparing stock for the stew we're having tonight."
I pull over a kitchen chair and climb up to watch.
"What's stock?" I ask.
"All the things you put in a good Irish beef stew," she tells me, pointing to the potatoes, carrots, and celery stalks lying on the kitchen counter. "It takes a good meat bone and lots of vegetables, and when you mix them in with the broth, they make a wonderful stew. Willie Peipert gave me the bone and choice pieces of beef when we went to his butcher shop the other day, remember?"

"Oh, yeah!" My mouth waters just at the thought of all the meat in Willie Peipert's butcher shop where Mom buys our meat at the Northside in Alton. He always reaches in the meat case with his glasses on top of his head, but they never fall off.

"Vegetables are good for you, too," Mom says.

At that, I screw up my nose, making Mom laugh.

"Come on, they're not that bad. I know you like celery. Here, see if you can cut this into small pieces," and she pulls a long piece from the stalk to show me. "Be careful now because the blade is sharp."

So my Mother and I go about making the stew, with Mom cutting up everything but the celery that I'm in charge of.

"Your Grandfather Morrissey likes this recipe because it's called Irish Stew. But it tastes just like any other stew to me," she tells me, as she brings meat out of the ice box.

"Is Grandpa Irish?"

"I'll say so!"

"Are Barb and me Irish?" I ask.

"You sure are. You get it from both sides of the family, the Morrisseys and the Kings."

"Who's a Morrissey?"

"Well, my name was Antoinette Morrissey before I married your Father. And your grandfather, E. J., is a Morrissey. His mother's name was Higgins, and that's a very Irish name, too."

"Is Pop Irish?"

"Yes, your Father's Irish and so are his parents. Grandma King's maiden name was Fitzgerald. You can't get much more Irish than that!" And Mom laughs just at the thought.

"So Pop's all-Irish?"

"Sure is."

"Are you all-Irish, too?"

My Mother stops slicing the meat and looks at me like she's grateful for the question. "No, I'm not all-Irish, Jean Ellen. My mother's family came from France and Germany. And John Blake, my grandfather, came from England." When Mom said this, her voice trailed off like a lone blade of grass waving in a field of shamrocks.

"So that's how you didn't get all-Irish?" I ask.

"Yep, that's how I didn't get all-Irish." Amused, she places the ingredients in the pot as I watch the boiling water lower to a simmer. "And Antoinette Blake, my grandmother, came from the Alsace Lorraine region of France." I perk up, hearing the name 'Antoinette.'

"Is that where you got your name?"

"Yes. People think I'm named after the Queen of France, Marie Antoinette, but I was really named after my grandmother." Mom looks at the celery pieces I have diligently cut. "You've got quite a pile there, Jean Ellen. Here, dump them in the pot." And she cups her hands, helping me scoop them up. "There, that should do it." Setting the stove to medium heat, she puts the lid on the pot and turns on the faucet. "Here, wash your hands. We'll stir it again in a few minutes."

"But wouldn't you know," Mom goes on, "some goof wrote 'Mary Antoinette' on my baptismal record instead of Marie Antoinette." From the disgust in my Mother's voice and the look on her face, I see she is still irked about it. I sit back down on the chair, eager to hear more.

Seeing my interest, she pulls up a chair alongside me. "Long ago, my great-grandparents came over here from France and Germany, and then...oh, I better write this down. It's hard enough for me to keep everyone straight let alone tell you. Here," she says, removing the lid off the pot and handing me a ladle, "get up and stir the stock while I write, but do it slowly." Then Mom reaches for her grocery list pad, and with a pencil, writes:

My side:
The Graessles came across the ocean from France and Germany
Antoinette, their daughter, came with them from France
Antoinette married John Blake who came from England
Their daughter, Barbara, was your grandmother
Barbara married E. J. Morrissey - your grandfather
They had a daughter, Antoinette - that's me!

Your Father's side:
The Kings and Fitzgeralds came from Ireland but we don't know which part
We don't know if your grandfather John King was born in Ireland, but your grandmother Josephine Fitzgerald was born in Alton
Your King aunts and uncles were all born in Alton - Uncle Mart, Uncle John, Aunt Margaret, and Aunt Ellen

Mom looks at what she has written, glances over at me, and bursts out laughing. "Oh, heavens, Jean Ellen! What on earth am I thinking of! You can't read writing yet, can you! Well, give this to Barbara. She'll print it for you."

But I'm still mulling over being Irish. "So Barb and me aren't all-Irish?"

"That's right, Jean Ellen," and Mom gives me a devilish grin. "And I'm the culprit!"

Slowly, I stir the stock, making circles around all the colorful vegetables, and each time the delicious smell of Irish stew escapes into the kitchen.

"By the way, did I ever tell you your great-great-grandparents, the Graessles, lived on William Street at the foot of Bond? But I never knew them because they died before I was born."

"Where'd everybody else live?"

"Right here in this house!"

"Everybody?" I gasp.

"Well, not all at once," Mom laughs, wholeheartedly. "The Graessles never lived here, but they're the ones who built the house for their daughter, Antoinette. When she died, my Mother inherited it, and after mom died, the house became mine and your Father's."

"Wow!"

"So just like the stew, your ancestors came from many places in the world to live in this house: France, England, Germany, and Ireland. We're a stew, all right, but not just an Irish one."

"A family stew?" I suggest.

"That's a good way of putting it," Mom laughs. Then she emphatically adds, "But any way you look at it, Jean Ellen, you and your sister come from good stock."

Satisfied with her conclusion, Mom turns the gas low under the stew, covers the pot, and hands me a dish cloth to help with drying the dishes.

My Mother Marie Antoinette (Annie) Morrissey King

SEVENTEEN MARIE ANTOINETTE MORRISSEY KING

If you come up Prospect Street hill, you'll see a large white frame house built circa 1850 in Queen Anne architectural style. My Mother's Alsatian great grandparents, Heinrich and Barbara Wertz Graessle, built it for their daughter, Antoinette Graessle Blake, and family members have lived in the house for over a hundred years until we moved in 1955. The house, like my Mother, was the hub of the family.

   Marie Antoinette Morrissey (Annette to some, Annie to our immediate family), embodied traits of her Irish, French, German and English ancestors; she was no pedigree. She loved the musical sound of the Irish brogue, favored French-style furniture, used German expressions and could, on occasion, possess an English reserve. She believed in the Christian God and followed the teachings of the

Catholic Church. Religion was the means by which she lived her spirituality, which was deep in her. The ritual and mystery in Catholic liturgy appealed to her contemplative leanings and strengthened her belief in the power of intercession.

Like her father, Edmund James Morrissey (E. J.), who had studied for the priesthood, she, too, considered being a nun, but her mother's early death in 1917, when Annie was seventeen, brought that aspiration to an end. She grew up fast as a consequence. Her new role put her in the incongruent situation as head of the family, being teenage mother to her two younger siblings, Barbara, fifteen, and Gene, eight, and of two older brothers, Jim and Ed. With a degree in business from the Ursuline Academy in Alton, she worked as part-time accountant at the family business, Morrissey Brothers Shoes (later, Morrissey-King Shoes), and was the only family member who conversed with neighbors on par with wives in the neighborhood. Quite a balancing act for a teenager to juggle.

Energetic and outgoing, Annie easily became the hub of the Morrissey household. She dated often, drove the family car, and boasted how a family friend, Arnold Gibson, declared her "the best driver in Alton" to which she added, "and he said not just a woman driver either!" A tall, lean, attractive woman, Annie took pride in her long black hair that she often parted down the middle, remarking that not many women could "wear their hair like that and look good." Still, she envied her husband Jimmie King's natural curly hair saying, "Wouldn't you know! The man gets curls and the woman's is straight as a poker!" Although she took pride in her good looks, she was self-deprecating to a fault. A person would be hard-pressed to find a picture of her in a family album where she had not scratched out her face.

After her marriage to James Joseph (Jimmie) King in 1932, Annie continued the open-door policy of the King home to neighbors, friends, and relatives who routinely came in and out during the day. To hear someone call out "Anybody home?" brought Annie out from the kitchen or down the stairs. She knew without seeing if it was her brother, Jim, from Springfield, by the smell of his cigar. If it was her brother, Ed, he walked straight to the back room to engage E. J. in "shop talk" about the day's business. If Gene arrived, he planted a kiss on his sister's cheek and headed for the kitchen ice box, helping himself to a bottle of beer. And if her sister, Barb, arrived from St. Louis, Annie stifled a laugh upon seeing her temperamental nephew, Virg, carrying his non-allergic pillow for an overnight stay.

Annie loved birds and took great pleasure in caring for them. She always had a canary caged in the house near a window. Aside from despising "those dern Jays and Starlings" because they "steal from other birds," she marveled at them all. The canary was her favorite domesticated bird and the cardinal her choice of the wild. She was adamant that the female was called a red bird—not a cardinal. Her love for birds fostered her hate for "those sneaky cats." She spared no broom if a feline even thought of chasing after a bird.

Snappy in speech but slow to judge, quick moving yet gentle, these attributes roughly describe my Mother. Mostly, though, Annie had a great sense of humor and was pleasant to be around. She laughed a lot and loved a funny story but was uncomfortable with off-colored jokes. Although sociable, she did not seek social gatherings; she was not a joiner. She never belonged to The Altar Society or any church organization. The heart of a very active family, she liked quiet.

Annie's faith was important to her, but she did not wear her religion on her sleeve, a quality which prompted her brother-in-law, Hugh Anderson, to remark, "If I ever become a Catholic, I want to be one just like Annie." Daily, she walked down Prospect Street hill to early Mass at the Old Cathedral, never mentioning to anyone in the family that she did. Still, she was not afraid to express her disagreement with the Catholic Church. Once she walked out during a homily at Mass because she didn't like "the fire and brimstone" emitting from the pulpit. "I'm going home and have a cup of coffee," she told the startled usher as she left the pew. She also felt it was best not to argue politics and religion because "someone always gets hurt," quietly adding, "those Republicans have never been for the little guy."

Annie and Jimmie King had two daughters, Barbara Blake and Jean Ellen. After her brother, Gene, tragically drowned in the Mississippi River in 1946, Annie and Jimmie renovated the second floor of their home into an apartment for Gene's widow, Helen, and her two children, Jean Louise and young Gene. And the Kings and Morrisseys became one family.

EIGHTEEN   DIAL 37531

It weighs a ton, the shiny, black telephone receiver that takes both my hands to lift. Hum goes the sound Mom calls the dial tone that tells me it's time to turn the numbers. Grunting, I struggle to hold the heavy receiver with one hand and dial with the other, but each time I try, the phone slips around on the telephone stand and I can't make the numbers work. "Oh, gosh," I mutter, exasperated, and plunk the receiver down on the floor. Bracing the phone with one hand and positioning my forefinger with the other, I dial 37531. Hurriedly, I pick the receiver up with both hands and listen. One ring, two rings, and then a pickup. A familiar voice comes over the wire.

"Morrissey-King Shoes," answers Uncle Ed. I grin, but remain silent. I haven't figured out yet that he can't see it's me. "Hello? This is Morrissey-King's," he repeats.

"Hullo, Uncle Ed," I finally respond.

"Oh, hi there, Jeanie. How you doin?"

"Okay." Silence again.

"Want to talk to your Father?"

"Yes, please."

"Hold on."

Since learning to dial our store's phone number, I find all sorts of excuses to do so. This time, it's to get new shoes for my sister who's starting kindergarten in the Fall. Well, not only for my sister, exactly. For me, too. In our house, one of us never gets a pair of shoes without the other. Not like with clothes. With them, I always get Barb's hand-me-downs. "Used to be Barbara's" is all I ever say when someone asks me where I got my new coat or new blouse or something. But never with shoes. Shoes always come new in our house. They're new and our own.

After a minute, Pop comes to the phone. "What is it, Jean Ellen?"

"Barbara needs new shoes!" I emphatically announce.

"She does, does she?" he asks, and I can hear the smile in his voice. "For any special reason?"

"Uh-huh. Kinergarn."

"Is that so? Well, I guess we'll have to do something about that, won't we, kiddo. You better put your Mother on the line."

"Okay." I drop the heavy receiver on the floor, run out of my parent's bedroom, and holler down the back steps to the kitchen. "Mom! Pop wants to talk to you on the phone right away!"

"All right, I'm coming. Don't hang up 'til I get it down here."

I scurry back to the bedroom, cautiously pick up the receiver, and eavesdrop. "Would it be just as easy for me to bring them home tonight?" my Father is saying.

"I have to get groceries at Horn's and go to the butcher's on the Northside anyway," Mom tells him. "We might just as well come on down to the store after that."

"Okay. But make it close to 5:00 if you can, honey. Been a busy day. What's for supper?"

"Nothing that can't wait. Meatloaf and left overs." Just then I accidentally drop the receiver on the floor. "Oh, gosh!" I whisper, and fall down next to it, pressing my ear against the ear piece.

"Hey, kiddo! You still there?" I hear my Father ask.

"Uh-huh."

"You want to come down to the store?"

"For shoes?"

Both parents laugh. "Yep, we're going to get your big sister ready for school. Glad you reminded us." They laugh again. "Maybe I better take a look at yours, too. Are your toes up to the edge yet?" I sit up and press my fingers into the tip of my shoes to feel my toes, just like I've seen my Father do with customers. Lying down, I yell into the mouthpiece.

"They're almost there, Pop!"

"Sounds like you'll need a new pair, too, kiddo."

"Okay, Jimmie," Mom interrupts. "We'll be down later."

So that afternoon, Mom buys fresh fruit and vegetables from the sidewalk stand at Horn & Horn's Grocery Store on State Street while Barb and I hang around the candy counter inside. Soon Cass Horn, the owner, reaches behind the glass counter and swoops up a handful of gum balls that he divides between us. "No charge," he whispers to his assistant as we juggle the balls in our hands. Minutes later, with our cheeks and pockets bulging, we ride on out to the Northside where Willie Peipert, the butcher, helps Mom select meat for supper. I stand silently chewing my gum ball, intrigued by Willie's glasses that he wears atop his bald head. When he hands Mom her purchases, he asks Barb and me if we'd like a slice of cheese.

"Yes, please," we answer in unison.

"What kind?"

"Swiss!" I immediately respond because I know it's my Father's favorite.

"Good heavens!" Mom suddenly exclaims, looking at her watch. "It's nearly 5 o'clock! Good-bye, Mr. Peipert." Then, reaching for the door, she asks us, "Did you girls thank Mr. Peipert for the cheese?" We do, and soon we're off again down State Street, pass Grace Updike's Confectionery so fast that I know it's useless to ask Mom to stop for candy. "Wait in the car while I put the meat in the ice box," she tells us as we pull up in front of our house. Up the sidewalk she hurries, and in a minute, she's back behind the wheel heading down Bond Street for town.

Passing Hayner Library, Mom tells Barb, "We'll get you a library card this year." I look over at the building that houses books that means words that means reading that means learning that means school. "Grandpa reads to me," I remind them. And this is the way I like it. With Gramps, I can make up the pictures in my mind as he tells me the story.

We're lucky. The downtown business district has cleared out, so Mom pulls up right in front of our store at 112 West Third Street. Barb and I run through the entrance and into our Father's arms. "Hey, look who's here!" he laughs, hugging us. Gramps comes out of his office, and Uncle Ed appears out of the stock room.

"Two new customers?" he asks, then looks down at our shoes. "Gee, I don't know if we've got big enough sizes for these feet!"

"Now, Edmund," Grandpa reprimands his son, "you mustn't speak to these little girls like you do to your boys."

After several tries, Barb and I both end up with a new pair of shoes. "These should last a while," Pop tells us, tossing them back in the box and handing it to us.

"Jim, you and Dad go ahead on home. I'll lock up," Uncle Ed offers. So off we go, shoe boxes underarm and without a care in the world—nor an inkling of how the approaching school year will alter our happy lives at home forever.

That evening, I follow the voices I hear in the dining room and see my parents and Grandpa pulling up chairs around the dining room table. "What you doing?" I ask, but no one replies, so I know it's something worth hanging around for. Grownups never tell you something unless they want to. Barb opens a paper pad and starts drawing circles over and over again. Standing at her elbow, I watch. It looks like rolled up barbed wire around our chicken coop to me, all those circles she's drawing. She and Gramps look so serious, too. I wait a few moments before asking, "What you doin' that for, Barb?"

but she doesn't even hear me she's working so hard, biting her lip as she draws on and on.

"I'm writing," she finally answers. I look from her face back to the paper, bewildered. All I see are rolls of barbed wire.

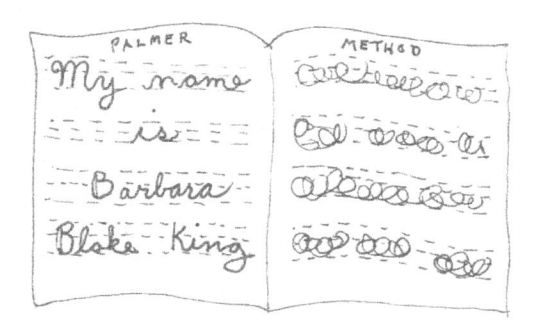

"See," she says, proudly holding up her practice book. "The halfway lines are for small letters, the big lines for capitals. It's called Palmer Method." Carefully, she repositions the book on the table, and resumes twirling. "Grandpa says I'll be able to write before I even start kindergarten," she proudly tells me. I shoot a look at Gramps who's intent upon her every move. He stops just long enough to look over his spectacles at me.

"In two years, you'll be learning the same, little girl. But now, you must be very quiet so your sister can concentrate on her letters." Seeing my dissatisfaction, he says, "Barbara, give Jean Ellen a paper. No harm in giving her a head start."

My sister tears off a piece and shoves it in front of me. Now I purse my lips, pick up a stubby pencil, and attempt to copy her circles, but I quickly lose interest. I can't imagine what all those rolls of wire are trying to say. Laying my head on my arm, I pensively watch my big sister draw on and on, an expression of utter clarity and purpose on her face.

I'll never get the hang of that, I think, feeling disheartened as I walk away from the table. The world of learning upon whose precipice I stand already appears uninviting.

Winter

Prospect Street in Winter (photo by Dr. Bill Malone)

NINETEEN   PROSPECT STREET

Fortified with a bowl of pablum under my belt, I race to the front hall steps for Mom to help me pull on my leggings.

"Wait for me, Barb!" I cry out to my big sister who already is opening the front door to go out.

"I can't," she tells me. "I'm sweltering with all these clothes on," and out the door she goes.

"Hold still!" Mom says, exasperated, as I squirm to catch up with my sister. "Once you set foot out in that snow, I won't see you again 'til the end of day, so you've got to bundle up good," she explains. I obey, just to hurry things along. "My fingers are so dern stiff today," she complains, more to herself than to me. I look down and see her swollen knuckles that the doctor calls arthritis as she struggles with

91

the zipper on my snowsuit, a hand-me-down from Barbara. To assure me, she says, "Barbara Blake won't go without you. Look, she's waiting on the porch."

But seeing my sister cleaning the new snow off my sled from last night's storm doesn't quiet me, it just sets me jumping again.

"Don't forget your mittens," Mom calls after me as I race to the door. I run back, grab them off the hall tree, and am off.

Jean Ellen and Barbara Blake

It's fun growing up on Prospect Street, especially in Wintertime. Once the season comes to our hilltop world, it stays. I can sled all day long in the snow that lasts from November to March, and sleep as sound as a bear above the town's distant bustle. Daytime whites and blues, afternoon golds, grays and browns fill my coloring book on days when the storm rages outside and Mom returns an emphatic "No!" to my pleadings to go out.

Today, as Barb and I traipse down Prospect Street, the black bark of trees, stripped of Summer foliage, lines the street in contrast to the houses draped in snow like icing on gingerbread. We're as bundled up in our snowsuits as the houses are in their blankets of snow. Overhead, dim Winter light filters through gray clouds holding the promise of another storm. I scrape my boot along the snow-covered street, trying to find the tire marks I made with my tricycle last Summer, but cars have packed the snow so hard, I barely make a dent in it.

A door opens, and Mrs. Dempsey waves to us as she hurriedly picks up her mail and scurries back inside. Soon she'll be sitting at her window where she sits most of the Winter, sipping tea and looking like she's dreaming. Across the street, a tap on the window reveals Idy, our housekeeper, waving her gnarled hand that's always red, Mom says, from dishwater. And even though I don't see our other neighbor, Mrs. Wuerker, I bet right now she's inside stretching her long, wrinkled neck with the choker around it, just to get a glimpse of who's walking down the middle of Prospect Street in the snow. As we pass Aunt Carrie and Uncle Will's, I try to tiptoe, which is hard to do in boots on the crunchy snow, because if my aunt sees us, for sure she'll holler out for me to bring her Mom's smelly sour milk that she loves to drink.

The crunch of snow under our boots not only announces to our neighbors that we're approaching, it also summons us to be part of the neighborhood. Living on Prospect Street is an adventure for each house looks different, each neighbor unique, each home inviting. Just as our house is located at the center of the street, I feel at the heart of the neighborhood.

Without speaking, my sister and I know where we're going once we reach the end of Prospect Street. We'll sled down steep Summit, our favorite spot, then walk from Bellevue (today's Belleview) to the Sunken Gardens at Riverview Park where the sledding's good and bumpy. After that, we'll wind down the Bailey side of the hollow, if the snow's not too deep, and then climb back up Summit for more sledding. Since our relatives, the Morrisseys, moved to Summit, we can show off as we sled past Aunt Helen who watches us from their picture window.

Getting to the top of Prospect and Summit, I strain to get a glimpse of the Mississippi, but I can't distinguish the river from the bank on the West Alton side. Closer still, the rise in the street to slow down cars between Rodger's and Schweppe's houses has disappeared. So I go to my walking encyclopedia, my sister, for answers.

"Where's the river?" I ask her.

"Under the ice."

"Where's the bump?"

"Under the snow."

"If I had my trike I wouldn't have to slow down at the bump, would I, Barb?"

"You couldn't ride your tricycle in the snow."

"Why?"

"Because the tires would make you slide all over. That's why we've got sleds with runners."

"Oh."

She pulls hers around now, positioning it so I can sit behind her. We usually go down steep Summit together sitting up, Barb in front steering with her feet and me behind holding on to her, with my sled tied to the back. We know I won't use mine until I learn to steer better, but I always bring it along, just in case. Today, though, feels different as I glance down Summit hill, so inviting in the fresh new snow, and I just stand there, hanging on to my sled.

As usual, Barb gets ready to sit, when all at once I get this urge, and before I know what I'm doing, bam! I hit the ground on top of my sled and skim down Summit belly-buster.

"Jean Ellen!" my sister screams at the top of her lungs, so loud that out of the corner of my eye I catch Aunt Helen framed in her window just in time to see me shoot like an arrow off the steepest part of the hill, fly straight down, clear the bottom, and change course up the other side.

Inside, my aunt races for the phone. "Annie!" she yells into the receiver to my Mother. "Do you know what your three-year-old daughter is doing?" She doesn't wait for an answer. "She just went down Summit Street on her sled all by herself—belly-buster!"

By the time my sled stops, Barb pulls up alongside me, and boy, is she ever mad. "You stupid thing!" she cries. "You could have been killed or something!"

But I can't help from grinning. Aren't I sitting here on my sled safe and sound and happy? She gets my message.

"Oh, all right, but next time you might not be so lucky."

Next time? I pull my sled around and start climbing up the hill as fast as I can. Next time, I'll steer up front and my big sister can sit in the back. And the very next time, I'll go belly-buster with only one hand, and wave at Aunt Helen with the other. And the very very next time, I'll just walk on down Prospect Street way ahead of my big sister, all by myself.

Ice cutter on the Mississippi River (photo by Dr. Bill Malone)

TWENTY   THE ICE CUTTERS

Suddenly, noises resound outside, crackling noises that boomerang up the hollow right into our house. From my bedroom, I scamper down the back steps to the kitchen and climb atop the radiator by the window to see. Yep, there it is, an ice cutter boat carving a pathway up the frozen Mississippi. Powered to undo the glacial world that entombs the waterway every Winter, these leviathans of the deep churn their mighty blades into a tympanic symphony, and in their wake, a fluid blue ribbon of Winter flows.

   I press my nose against the window, straining to see 'round the bend the inevitable coal-bearing barge that comes lumbering up the Mississippi in the aftermath of the cutter. And I'm not disappointed. A massive steel flatbed carrying rich, black coal appears, as a tiny white tugboat stealthily maneuvers it through the passageway. I sit back and watch them crawl past, almost as imperceptibly as the current itself, silent movers on the watery highway. With my finger,

I measure on the frosted windowpane where the tug begins and the barge ends, baffled by how they can fit in our window. Again, I lean forward, this time pressing my ear against the window, hoping to hear echoes of another cutter approaching in the distance, but the Mississippi is quiet now. Mesmerized by the sound that still swirls in my ears, I stare at the panoramic view created by the gulf in the bluffs out our kitchen window, and at the vast white world that covers Alton in Wintertime.

A steel blue sky, clear as the sharp December air, hangs overhead where, upriver, a sandbar of cloud veils the late afternoon sun. Wistfully, I raise my wrist to my lips, rubbing gently the soft, silky hair, a feeling that always comforts me. Warmth from the radiator makes me drowsy, and as I close my eyes, I feel like I'm sliding down a make believe hill on my sled.

From behind, someone asks, "Jean Ellen's glued to that window again?" and I hear my Mother laugh.

"Can't keep her away most of the Winter," she replies. I hear the ice box door open. "Here, Gene, I saved you a piece of pie." My eyes spring open, and I twist around to see Mom bringing out what's left of the lemon meringue pie from last night's supper. I'm off the radiator, and the ice cutters become a memory.

"Oh, oh!" she exclaims. "Little pitchers have big ears!"

I know that Mom's remark, a favorite among the adults in our household, refers to me, but, at five years of age, I don't comprehend its meaning, nor do I care—my eyes are riveted on the pie she now sets upon the counter. The meringue jiggles as she scoops up a huge piece with a spatula and deftly places it on a plate for my uncle.

"Mmmm, Annie, glad you saved that last big piece for me!" Uncle Gene exclaims, kissing Mom on the cheek as he grins mischievously at me. She laughs again, but I look on helplessly. Just remembering the sweet, tangy lemon at last night's supper sets my mouth watering all over again. But Uncle Gene is a favorite in our family, and even a five-year-old knows when the odds are against her. Still, I follow at his elbow as he gingerly walks to the kitchen table and places the pie ceremoniously upon it. "Like to keep me company, Jean Ellen?" he asks, pulling up a chair for me, then taking his own. I nod, and scurry up on it. That's when I see that my uncle has placed the pie directly in front of me. Slowly, he lifts his fork, cuts off a piece, slips it in his mouth and rolls it around and around, winding his face so far from one side to the other that I think it might fall off. I swallow just to get it over with. Finally, he looks at me, and for an instant, the twinkle in his eyes disappears. "Jean Ellen," he says, waving the empty fork at me, "I hope you appreciate what a good baker your Mother is!" Then, turning to her, he adds, "Annie, I believe this is the best pie you've ever made!" A groan escapes me. I can't help it. But it doesn't matter 'cause Uncle Gene's all hunched up now and going at the pie again. And this time he doesn't savor it, he devours it. In fact, I think he's even forgotten he invited me to keep him company.

I hang in though, because I've learned that keeping quiet is the only hope I have in winning my uncle over, though I admit that right now it doesn't look too good for me. All of a sudden, as if he just noticed I was sitting there, he says, "Hey, Annie, you wouldn't happen to have another fork over there, would you?" I hold my breath, and before I can say scat, Mom's put a fork in my hand, and I've scooped up the last piece and put it on the plate she holds for me. "Little pitchers have big appetites," my uncle says, a trace of annoyance in his voice. But I pay no mind.

"Here," Mom tells Uncle Gene, "this'll satisfy you," and the aroma of fresh perked coffee fills the kitchen.

Suddenly I scoot off the chair with the meringue wobbling all the way back to the window. "I think I hear the cutters!" I cry out.

Out the window barges travel easily upriver, for the ice cutters have done their work. Through the frosty meringue, I trace my fork like a blade, then make jags down the side of the gooey lemon. When the blade slices through the hard crust on the bottom hitting the plate, I hear the crack of cutters all over again as I sit here eating pie atop the radiator in our kitchen overlooking the Mississippi.

CHRISTMAS

The cedar perfume
Slowly winds up the stairs
Like incense at Mass
Where we first must prepare

For THE DAY! Christmas morning
The best of the year
Santa! The tree!
All of us here!

As I steal down the stairs
Peeking out to my right
In the corner I see
My new Monarch bike

The lights on the tree
Fill the room like a stage
And under its branches
My presents all lay

He *Came*! Oh, He *Came*!
What a grandiose feeling!
It runs through my body
My head, it sends reeling

In haste, we tear
Out the door, down the street
"We'll just sing Mass faster
Skip a few beats!"

Home once again
With our gifts we now open
Santa'd brought all and more
Than we'd hoped for

Then as I look
To his chair by my bike
I see Santa's remnants
He'd eaten last night

His match! Sure he used it!
For burnt it did lay
The stool for his feet
Lay askew where he stayed

Quickly I run to his chair
Softly pressed
I see where he sat
A few moments to rest

My parents, they watch
As I happily dance
Around the twin parlors
And twirl in a trance

"Merry Christmas!" they wish me
And Pop swings me high
I feel like a reindeer
Way up in the sky!

Then gently he lowers me
Down to the floor
'Twas then that I notice
My crib, nothing more

I walk over slowly
My breath will not come
For right there before me
Lay Jesus, new born

"This is Christmas," Mom whispers
As I gaze at the scene
"The birthday of Jesus
Is what it all means."

All Seasons

A GUY FOR ALL SEASONS
Le Siffleur (The Whistler)

You're a guy for all seasons, standing there so jauntily, your mouth set in bronze forever playing a tune on your lips. Someone sure named you right because that's all you ever do, just stand there with your hands in your pockets, whistling.

I like to run my fingers around the cap on your head, and down over the high cheekbones that stand out from your lean, chiseled face. I stop at your mouth and turn an ear towards it. Is it "Playmate" you're whistling? "Playmate, come out and play with me." Yeah, that's it, I hear it clearly now. But how come you expect a song like that to work? You can't play outdoors. You can't even move your feet off the platform. Someone's got you stuck there for all seasons.

You don't mind if I trace my fingers down your swarthy neck and over your shoulders, do you? I like the way your clothes just hang, shirt all rumpled, pants baggy, even one leg's all rolled up nearly to your knee.

Before someone put you here in our front parlor, I bet you were out fishing or working on a barge, or having fun just whistling and ambling along the bank down by the Mississippi. I'm glad you didn't stop whistling, though, 'cause I can see it makes you happy, and from what I'm hearing, you sure know how to make a tune.

Feel me wandering down your legs, pressing the muscle around your turned up pants and tucking my fingers in between your toes? For sure, you were a tough outdoors guy 'cause you don't even have scratches on your feet from walking on the riverbank. You'd probably show me how to fish if I asked you, but I don't think fishin'd be much fun. I don't ever want to catch a smelly ol' fish.

Like how'd you ever get the same color clothes and skin? I bet you never have to change 'em or even take a bath. I bet you never have to do anything but whistle all day long in the sun.

I'd like to pick you up and carry you out to the front porch so I can hear you whistle while I play, but Mom's already warned me you're too heavy for me to lug around. Besides, I know that if I dropped you, it'd be curtains for us both.

You see, you're very special around here, guess 'cause you've got that very extraordinaire name, *Le Siffleur*.

How'd you get that, anyway? And how'd you come here to our house in the first place? Someone bring you all the way from the French country just so you could stand so proud, whistlin' "Play Mate" night and day in our very own parlor?

Who'd bring you all the way just to do that?

Cousins Ann and Jean at work
Photo by Marilyn Morrissey

Child's Play in the Seasons is our third project. In 2023 Jean wrote *Knowing the place....* And in 2015 we produced *Family Album and Trilogy*, a feature length film. How are we related? Our grandfathers, Will and E.J. Morrissey, were brothers.

ACKNOWLEDGEMENTS

Thanks to Ann Morrissey Davidson for believing in me, and for her creative drawings and layout of this book.

And to Judy Watts for her editing expertise and insightful comments. Her understanding, that the artistic *process* is equal to the final *product*, is rare and invaluable.